Asking the question, "H̶̶̶̶̶̶̶̶̶̶̶̶̶̶̶̶̶̶̶̶̶̶̶̶̶̶̶̶̶̶̶̶̶̶" counterintuitive, but I have seen too many students on fire to change the world for Jesus get to seminary and become overwhelmed educationally, relationally, and spiritually. That's why I'm so excited about this book! It addresses how to survive in all these areas and more! Want to enter and graduate seminary on fire for Jesus? Get this book!

-JONATHAN AKIN
Director for Young Leader Engagement
North American Mission Board

This guide is a great read, full of "snap, crackle, and pop." It's edgy, pushy, and intrusively granular, but unmistakably amiable. And though it is written pointedly for the seminarian, much of it applies across the board to Christ's disciples in every walk of life. I found myself cheering (e.g., over their insistence on selfless, engaged churchmanship during seminary days and their praise for the bi-vocational approach). But sometimes I had to swallow hard (e.g., at places in the time-management section, as when they "slandered" TV). As I heard one fellow tell a pastor, "I couldn't 'Amen' when you preached, because it's hard to yell, 'Sic em,' when the dog's got you by the ankle." It's such a fine pastoral book, but when I say "pastoral," don't hear "sweetly clerical" as much as you hear "prophetically hygienic."

-MARK T. COPPENGER
Professor of Christian Philosophy and Ethics
The Southern Baptist Theological Seminary

Here is a book with practical and spiritual guidance in navigating the seminary years of education. It will answer questions you've wondered about, and it will provide answers to questions you haven't even thought to ask yet! Wisdom for the journey.

-TREVIN WAX
Bible and Reference Publisher at LifeWay Christian Resources
author of *This Is Our Time* and *Gospel-Centered Teaching*

Seminary students today have it harder than one might think. *The Complete Seminary Survival Guide* gives uncommon but wise counsel on how to navigate the spiritual, financial and academic challenges of graduate theological study. I gladly recommend this timely and helpful book!

–ART RAINER
Author of *The Money Challenge*
Vice President for Institutional Advancement
Southeastern Baptist Theological Seminary

The Complete Seminary Survival Guide is a great collection of practical wisdom for seminary students. Prospective and current seminary students face a host of challenges, and this book is a handy guide to doing seminary well.

–CRAIG GARRETT
Dean of Students and Assistant Prof. of Counseling
New Orleans Baptist Theological Seminary

This book addresses many of the challenges a seminarian will face during his years of study. The author shares clearly, and in many instances, persuasively, his counsel and perspective on these important issues. Anyone reading this book will be aided and helped by his ideas and suggestions.

–DANIEL L. AKIN
President, Southeastern Baptist
Theological Seminary

{The Complete}

SEMINARY SURVIVAL GUIDE

{The Complete} SEMINARY SURVIVAL GUIDE

START SMART | AVOID BURNOUT
FINISH STRONG

by Mark Warnock

Foreword by Jimmy Scroggins

The Complete Seminary Survival Guide

© 2017 by Mark Warnock

All rights reserved. No part of this work may be reproduced or disseminated in any form without the permission of the author, except as provided for by the copyright laws of the United States of America.

Published by
Seminary Survival Strategies
West Palm Beach, Florida
www.seminarysurvivalguide.com

For bulk purchase information for education or retail, contact mark@seminarysurvivalguide.com

Design: Seth Carter

Copy Editor: Chris Bonts

Scripture quotations marked (ESV) are from the ESV® Bible (The Holy Bible, English Standard Version®), copyright © 2001 by Crossway, a publishing ministry of Good News Publishers. Used by permission. All rights reserved.

Scripture quotations marked (NIV) are taken from the Holy Bible, New International Version®, NIV®. Copyright © 1973, 1978, 1984, 2011 by Biblica, Inc.™ Used by permission of Zondervan. All rights reserved worldwide. www.zondervan.com The "NIV" and "New International Version" are trademarks registered in the United States Patent and Trademark Office by Biblica, Inc.™

Printed in the United States of America

ISBN-13: 978-1977817891

ISBN-10: 1977817890

Contents

Foreword xi

Introduction xiii

- START SMART -

How to Pick a Seminary 1

Make Sure You're Supposed to Be at Seminary 7

Which Seminary Degree Should I Get? 13

Your Seminary Isn't Responsible for Your Education 17

Live Off Campus 21

Avoid the "Seminary Church" 23

- MANAGE YOUR TIME -

Seminary Survival Skill # 1: Triage 29

Map Out Your Degree 35

Syllabus Strategies for a Successful Semester 39

Planning Your Week: The Time Map 45

Tips for a Productive Day at Seminary 51

Master Your Seminary's Required Reading in Half the Time (or Less) 55

No One Cares What Your Grades Are 61

- MANAGE YOUR MONEY -

Learn How Money Works 67

How to Graduate Debt Free 71

Manage Your Money Wisely 77

Give Yourself a Raise 83

- AVOID TIME WASTERS -

Seminary Time Waster #1: Procrastination 93

Seminary Time Waster #2: The Digital Black Hole 99

Be Unavailable, Like Jesus. 103

Fix All Your Time Problems with One Decision 107

- STRENGTHEN RELATIONSHIPS -

The Hidden Spiritual Danger of Seminary 113

Relationships Are More Important Than You Think 119

Single at Seminary 123

Protecting Your Marriage at Seminary 127

- AVOID PITFALLS -

Stumbling at Seminary: Cheating 133

Stumbling at Seminary: Laziness 139

Stumbling at Seminary: Sexual Sin 145

- WHAT SEMINARY MAY NOT TEACH YOU -

Deciding Where You Stand 153

Navigating Seminary as a Woman 157

Learn to Share the Gospel 163

Learn to Love People 169

Ministry Is for Broken People 173

When You Should Quit 177

Acknowledgements 181

Further Resources 181

About the Author 183

Notes 185

x

Foreword

by Jimmy Scroggins

As a seminary student, professor, and dean, I have interacted with thousands of seminary students. Many of them have performed well, but many have struggled, flailed about, and ultimately failed. Their downfall was not due to lack of opportunity or aptitude, but rather to having wrong expectations or lack of ability to manage the complex challenges of seminary.

This is where The Complete Seminary Survival Guide comes in. This guide contains practical, actionable steps that will help seminary students balance the demands of higher education, finances, family, church, and personal character. It is easy to read and combines wise pastoral counsel with helpful "life hacks" to help readers succeed in school and, ultimately, in ministry.

It is my joy to be a pastor to Mark Warnock. Mark serves on our Family Church team giving pastoral oversight to our worship ministry and residency program. So far, he has earned two seminary degrees, most recently completing his Ph.D. at The Southern Baptist Theological Seminary while serving full time on our staff. He is a master time manager and compassionate leader with a heart to pass on what he has learned to others in ministry.

We all know that a seminary degree is only part of what prepares us for the work of ministry. But it is my hope that this book will find its way into the hands of many young men and women who are looking to impact our world with the gospel of Jesus. I truly believe that any seminarian who puts into practice the principles found here will excel in their education, and greatly enhance their future ministry potential.

DR. JIMMY SCROGGINS
Lead Pastor
Family Church

Introduction

Seminary is hard.

Seminary is hard *academically*. A Master's level education in theology, biblical studies and ministry is no cake walk. Compared to your undergraduate program, the reading load is heavier, the writing demands are greater, and the thinking required is more difficult and abstract.

Seminary is hard *financially*. The cost of higher education has skyrocketed in recent decades, and sadly, seminary is no exception. Additionally, most seminary students are young adults. Many are married, and quite a few have kids. Available jobs for seminarians don't typically pay much, and financial aid is scarce.

Seminary is hard *relationally*. If you move any distance to start seminary, the chances are that you will arrive with no friends or family nearby. You will be missing a big part of your relational support network. Rebuilding a new support network from scratch will take considerable time—time you are unlikely to have because of the crazy time demands of working while pursuing graduate study. Many seminary students struggle to find time just for the basic stuff of life: time with their spouses and children, time with God, time to just breathe! Where will you find time to building lasting relationships outside of your immediate family?

Seminary is hard *spiritually*. You come to seminary because you love God and want to serve him. You want to know the Bible better and be equipped. Studying the New Testament for class, however, is different from studying with a campus ministry group. The joy of discovering truth can fade under the weight of technical academic work.

Seminary will probably not be what you expect. Some students expect a three-year spiritual high, like a Passion Conference or revival meeting, and are disappointed when seminary turns out to be spiritually dull at times. Some expect close, fatherly mentoring from attentive professors. A few find that; most don't. Some expect an intellectual feast, course after course of sumptuous theological fare. It's a feast all right, but your part is to work like a prep cook in a hot kitchen, not sit at the table and enjoy.

Seminary might be the most demanding season of an aspiring minister's life.

In 2007, I started SeminarySurvivalGuide.com because there were several young men in my congregation who were called to ministry. My pastor and I had to repeat the same counsel to each of them about calling, ministry preparation, and the ins and outs of seminary. After posting regularly for about three years, I had said what I needed to say, and left the site inactive and almost untouched while I returned to seminary for doctoral study.

Since that time, I have been astonished by the enduring appeal of an inactive site, as each month hundreds of visitors still browse and read through old articles. That interest prompted me to collect the most helpful material, revise it, and put it into book form.

I write as a seminary survivor, having earned both my M.Div. and Ph.D. from highly regarded evangelical seminaries. I loved seminary and greatly benefitted from my time there. My enthusiasm for seminary is tempered, however, by the experience of over twenty years in local church ministry, which, to be honest, has made me something of a pragmatist. I also teach at a Christian college, and train church planters out of a church-based residency program. As a result, I have been able to see seminary from three distinct perspectives: that of a pastor, a professor, and a student. Out of these experiences, I have reflected on how and to what degree seminary really prepares you for ministry.

Think of this book like a travel guide, a Fodor's or Lonely Planet handbook to seminary. It points out the highlights and must-see elements, steers you away from dangerous areas, and, most importantly, advises you on how to get the most out of the experience. I intentionally challenge conventional wisdom and take provocative stances, not because my ideas are always right or best, but because I want to challenge your thinking and stir you to find solutions that work *for you*.

Most of all, however, I want you to survive seminary. The church desperately needs more godly, qualified leaders. Seminary is a daunting hurdle for those preparing for ministry, and is almost never what you expect. I want to help you get through with your ministry, your family, your finances, and your soul intact.

How to Read This Book

Do not read this book from beginning to end. You're not here to serve this book; this book is here to serve you. Start in the Table of Contents, and browse through whatever chapters seem most appealing to you. Read what you want, take the best, and ignore the rest.

In many chapters, I direct you to extra resources, links, and bonus materials at the website. They can all be found at seminarysurvivalguide.com/book-extras.

Seminary is a gift, a rare opportunity that many people in the world never get. Let's talk about how to make the most of it.

> "Be very careful, then, how you live—not as unwise but as wise, making the most of every opportunity, because the days are evil" (Ephesians 5:15-16, NIV).

MARK WARNOCK
West Palm Beach, Florida

START SMART

I
How to Pick a Seminary

Choosing a seminary is no small decision, because it will be a significant investment of your life. It will take years, it will cost tens of thousands of dollars, and it will be a challenge. Give careful thought as you make your choice.

The first truth to remember is that seminary is not an end in itself. It is a means to prepare you for ministry. So from the beginning, ask yourself: what kind of ministry will I be doing? Even if you're not entirely certain, your plans for future ministry will influence which seminary might be the best choice for you.

Here are several factors to consider as you're choosing a seminary. Some factors are more important (doctrine) than others (special programs).

Denomination. Do you belong to a particular denomination? If you're committed to serve a particular arm of the church, start with their seminaries. Southern Baptist students will probably gravitate to one of the six SBC seminaries. Presbyterian Church in America students may choose to attend Covenant Seminary in St. Louis or Reformed Theological Seminary in Jackson or Orlando. If you aren't tied to a particular denomination, or will be working in parachurch movements, you have more options.

Doctrine. Seminaries vary in their doctrine, so know your seminary's confessional position before you go. Seminary education provides a credential for your resume that will label you as being one of "their kind" of students. Of course, it is possible to be a liberal student at a conservative school, or vice versa, but if you want to establish conservative credentials, for instance, going to a liberal school will probably work against you.

Faculty. The quality of instruction at a seminary is directly linked to the quality of the faculty. Some seminaries are loaded with well-known, published scholars. Others have credentialed but unknown professors. Is there a scholar you absolutely want to study with? Keep in mind that reputation is not an entirely reliable guide. A professor whose academic work is highly respected may be crummy in the classroom. Some of the most able teachers might be people you've never heard of.

Culture. Every seminary has its own culture and emphasis. What are the schools you're considering known for? Academic theology? Apologetics? Missions and evangelism? Social engagement?

Location. One downside of residential seminaries is that often you must move to a new city and leave the region where you intend to serve upon graduation. This separation can last for years, which disconnects you from the local culture, ministry network, and established family relationships where you currently live. Always give careful consideration to local options before you move across the country.

Cost. How much will this education cost you? This consideration is critically important because vocational ministry does not pay very well on average. Student loans can become a serious financial millstone around your neck. Many prospective seminary students already have significant debt from their undergraduate work. Our prayer is that seminary will not create additional debt for you.

We contacted several seminaries and asked them to approximate the expense of earning a degree with them. This information turned out to be difficult to find. Websites were unhelpful. Some admissions departments were evasive. Our investigation found that the average tuition for a Master of Divinity from a reputable, accredited, evangelical seminary in 2017 is around $50,000. Some are higher. The cost of seminary has soared along with all other higher education. Even after adjusting for inflation, seminary tuition is around 40% higher than it was a generation ago. Keep in mind, this figure is for tuition only — it does not include books, fees or other expenses.

Some denominational seminaries offer large discounts to students from their denomination, as much as 50% or more, which is a significant advantage. A few seminaries with large endowments even offer tuition-free seminary. Before you rush to apply, however, consider other factors, like the doctrine and culture of the school. In terms of your final ministry goal, a free Master of Divinity from a seminary outside your confession might prove to be a major obstacle to your future employment in the church. Some of these free programs come from declining denominations desperate for a new generation of leaders. Also, some "free seminary" programs are not accredited. They may not meet the same academic standards, and may not be recognized as a legitimate credential. Investigate carefully before enrolling.

Special programs. Some seminaries may offer special concentrations not available in other places: urban ministry, cross-cultural missions, women's ministry, and leadership. Again, think about your future ministry as you evaluate the availability of these programs.

Availability of jobs while in seminary. A seminary in a small town may not provide the kind of employment opportunities you need to support yourself as easily as other locations. Ask if your seminary has any special relationships with local employers.

Online seminary or distance options. Nearly every seminary has online or distance options now. Some seminaries have regional satellite locations where you can attend class without moving, or offer modular courses where you only go to campus for one- or two-week intensives. Online classes can be a good choice, if you have the kind of discipline necessary to study where you are. Some students do better when they are in the physical environment of seminary.

Online or distance options open up more employment possibilities, too. You might be able to earn more money at a local business or church ministry position than working part-time at UPS or Starbucks in a new town. Online seminary can also move with you from town to town. If you have a job that requires travel, or are doing ministry already in a remote location, online seminary might be a good choice.

Alternatives to seminary. Look for local churches that have residency programs for pastors or church planters. While these options aren't plentiful, increasing numbers of seminaries are partnering with churches to provide credit for church-based ministry training. These programs sometimes cost significantly less than residential seminaries as well.

Pray. "The heart of man plans his way, but the Lord establishes his steps" (Proverbs 16:9, ESV). God knows your future far better than you. Ask him. Like a good shepherd, you can expect that he will guide you right. Depend on it.

Extras:

Go to seminarysurvivalguide.com/book-extras for extra resources, including a two-page guide to choosing a seminary.

2
Make Sure You're Supposed to Be at Seminary

Not everyone is supposed to be in ministry. Not everyone is supposed to be in seminary.

This may seem a little insulting as a starting point, but hang with me for a bit.

Many high school graduates go to college without really knowing what they want to do. They spend semesters changing majors and trying to find themselves, incurring a pile of debt along the way. It would have saved them lots of money and effort had they taken the time sort out their direction for life before enrolling.

In the same way, seminary is not the place to explore whether you are called to ministry. It's not a good place to get smarter about the Bible while you contemplate your options. Save yourself the money and time and be sure your calling to ministry is firm before you start.

Seminary will test your true fitness for a life of ministry. The multiple stresses of seminary function much like Organic Chemistry does for would-be med students. It's a "weeding out" class. Not everyone is cut out for med school. Many times, flunking Organic Chemistry is how they get the message.

Unfortunately, the weeding out process for ministry isn't as clear cut as a poor grade in a critical class. The true weeding out happens gradually, and often painfully. Over the years I've met many who shouldn't have been in ministry, and the signs were obvious. Unfortunately for the church and their families they were unable to see the signs until they had done much harm to both.

For many Christians and churches, the idea of divine calling to ministry isn't understood very well. It's mysterious and a little subjective. When someone in the church claims to have a call of God on their lives to lead in ministry, people usually don't question it. They accept it uncritically, and assume the person announcing such a calling is right.

And admittedly, it's not easy to measure genuine calling from God and fitness for ministry. There's no quick test for it.

But that does not mean discerning whether or not someone is called is unimportant. A divine calling to ministry is real, it comes from God, and mature believers in Christ can rightly discern it. It's also important. A person who wants to lead in Christian ministry ought to have a divine call on their lives that goes beyond the general call to ministry that every Christian receives when they decide to follow Christ.

There are generally two realities that are true of people who are genuinely called by God to do vocational ministry.

They are certain enough of their own calling to pursue it.

There is a bit of mystery with regard to how this calling is experienced. God speaks and moves in mysterious ways. But every individual I've known in ministry has a story of how they came to sense the calling of God in their lives to go into ministry.

For my friend Josh, his call to ministry came while studying John Piper's book, *Don't Waste Your Life*. He looked hard at what a meaningful life in God's eyes really was and compared it to his own. Josh had a great job he loved with a fantastic salary, but in light of eternity, it didn't seem very significant. So he resigned, moved his family to seminary, and now serves as a missionary in South America.

My call to ministry happened during a summer mission experience when my team served in various churches for 10 weeks. Halfway through the summer, the growing sense in my heart was that I couldn't do anything else with my life, that leading God's people was what I was supposed to do. It was cemented in a moment of prayer in the Scriptures by a poolside in Orlando, Florida. I remember it like it was yesterday. My questions and fears were greeted by answers and assurances from God's word.

Do you have a story you can tell about your own calling? How specific is it? How definite is it? When you encounter difficulties in ministry — and believe me, you will — many times the only thing that will sustain you is an inward confidence that God has spoken, that you have heard, and that vocational ministry is His plan for your life.

Other believers see the calling on their lives and affirm it.

I once knew a pastor who thought he was called to pastor because he had an emotional experience at a conference. But many others and I could tell that he should not have been in ministry. Three weeks after he started pastoring his church, his people began asking all kinds of questions. They ranged from, "Is everything all right with him?" to "How do you fire a pastor?" Three weeks was all it took for the lack of a call to become obvious.

Over the next two years, his ministry unraveled, and he was forced out of the church. It was ugly for the church, for the staff, and especially for he and his family. As it turned out, two other churches had previously forced him out. For some reason, he never woke up and saw what was so obvious to everyone else.

Spare yourself the grief of a failed ministry that is not initiated by God. Spare the church of God. Be certain of your calling. Seek wise counsel from honest friends and church leaders who know God well and know you well. Pray together and sound out your calling. Ask if they can see evidence of the inward calling you have experienced. You want more voices in this group than just your mom or sweet grandma who thinks everything about you is amazing. External confirmation from serious men and women of God will reinforce and authenticate your inner sense of calling. Later, when times of doubt come, you can go back to how the Holy Spirit spoke through the Body of Christ to affirm God's calling on your life.

Extras:

Go to <u>seminarysurvivalguide.com/book-extras</u> for extra resources, including a two-page calling assessment, plus links to other resources on calling.

3
Which Seminary Degree Should I Get?

A seminary degree is valuable in two ways. First, it has value because it prepares you for ministry. Second, it has value because it provides you with credentials that testify to your qualification for ministry. So which degree should you get?

The Master of Divinity (M.Div.) is the standard, time-honored degree for pastors and other leaders in the church. It includes biblical and theological studies as well as a range of coursework in the practical aspects of ministry like preaching, pastoral care, evangelism, and administrative responsibilities. In a sense, it's two degrees in one, and it has the benefit of being comprehensive. The down side? At around 90 credit hours, it will take three to four years of full-time study to complete.

Most seminaries, however, now offer shorter degree options in biblical studies, theology, Christian ministry or Christian education. The options may come with an emphasis in student ministry, urban ministry, missions, church planting or preaching. Think very strategically about this question: Is the value of the M. Div. sufficient to warrant an extra 1-2 years of full-time study to get it?

Several seminaries I'm aware of really encourage (some might say push) students toward the M.Div. Some even make you sign a statement that you aren't planning to go into pastoral ministry if you enroll in a shorter degree program, which they say is designed for lay people.

Ministry Preparation

If it's an option for you, compare the shorter degree to the longer one. Put the curriculum lists side by side, and see exactly what you'd miss by pursuing the shorter degree. Ask fellow students about the value of the courses in the longer degree program. Will you really be better prepared for ministry with the extra classes or are they needless hurdles for you to jump through?

A trend I hope to see catch on pairs a two-year degree in biblical and theological studies with a multi-year internship with an established and thriving church. The practical side of ministry is learned hands-on, under the supervision of experienced mentors, instead of in a classroom. The disadvantage is that it can be hard to find such internship opportunities, although they are becoming more common.

Credential

For many churches, the fact that you get a degree from seminary is all that matters. They don't care what the degree is. Other churches may be more particular about it. Think ahead to your ministry work. If you can spend two years less and get the same credential without sacrificing real value in ministry preparation, then you might seriously consider a shorter program. You can save a lot of money that way, too.

When I was in seminary, I seriously considered a shorter program, the M.A. in Theology. Ultimately, however, I decided to stick with the M. Div. For me, it was the right choice, but not because I needed all the additional coursework in the M.Div. What I really needed was time to mature both personally and spiritually, and to gain ministry experience. Many times, when we feel called to ministry, we want to get to the ministry field as quickly as possible, so our mantra becomes "save time, save time." In the Christian life, however, sometimes the wisest thing you can do is to take your time. My maturity could not be rushed. I needed the time the longer degree took to really prepare myself spiritually for ministry.

Find out what your options are, and talk with your seminary's admissions counselors. They have conversations all the time with students making the same choice that you are, and are familiar with the issues that come with choosing one program over another.

As with all major decisions, seek godly counsel from mature friends and mentors.

Most importantly: pray over this decision. For all my urgings for you to be wise, remember that the fear of the

Lord is the beginning of wisdom. God knows your future and which path is best for you. Seek Him on it and obey.

Bottom line: Don't just pick a default degree because it's tradition, because everyone else does it, or because your seminary is pushing it. Give the decision serious, intentional thought and prayer.

Extras:

Go to <u>seminarysurvivalguide.com/book-extras</u> for extra resources.

4
Your Seminary Isn't Responsible for Your Education

Your seminary isn't responsible for your education. You are.

Some current and just-graduated seminarians told me this about their seminary experience:

- The seminary environment is too academic.
- The assigned readings are too long, and not really related to the subject matter.
- If I do everything they ask me to, I won't have a life at all.
- How can I learn to pastor from professors who've never pastored?

Most seminaries are built on an academic model, focused on seeing that you master a theological knowledge base in an insulated environment removed from the real world of ministry.

One recent graduate remarked, "It's one thing to talk in class about the practice of church discipline, it's another thing to do it sitting down and looking people in the eye." The disconnect he saw and lamented was that the ones teaching church discipline in class had never actually had to do it.

Which leads me to emphasize again, seminary does not prepare you for ministry. Not by itself. The traditional seminary environment can only provide one (albeit very important) piece of the total picture of your ministry preparation. Seminary grants to you a theological foundation and provides a credential supporting your desire and calling to serve in ministry.

The rest is up to you. You must take responsibility for your own ministry preparation.

- You will need real world experience in ministry, so go get some.
- You will need a mentor in your field, so go find one.
- You will need to be with people outside the Christian bubble, so go make some new friends.

If you immerse yourself in the seminary environment in the way students are tacitly encouraged to--reading every book, completing every assignment, and focusing on the subject matter presented in class, two things will happen. First, you will have spent years isolated from the world around you and will be unaccustomed to living with the real, lost people to whom you have been sent to minister. Second, it is highly likely that you will emerge as a theological egghead, with lots of knowledge but not much love.

Another student I spoke with, no doubt in the middle of mid-term madness, was aghast at how excessively his professors overburdened him with readings, papers, and assignments. "No one could do all this and have a real life," he complained.

My reply? Don't do every assignment. Go have a real life. You must set your own life agenda, just as you will have to when you're serving a church. If you allow the institution to dictate your life, it probably will not be the life you want or need.

Questions to consider as you balance life and seminary education:

- Are you fully plugged into the life of a local church?
- Do you know your pastors well? Do they know you?
- Are you serving in your church?
- Have you sought out someone more experienced in ministry for mentoring?
- What exposure do you have to people who are far from God? Unless you plan to stay buried in an irrelevant Christian ghetto the rest of your life, you need to make being with lost friends part of the fabric of your life.
- When's the last time you ignored an assignment in order to do something more important?

Try this exercise:

Sit down with a blank sheet of paper and design for yourself, from scratch, a ministry preparation program. Make three columns.

> Knowledge: What do you need to know?

Skill: What do you need to be able to do?

Experience: What kind of experience will you need?

Then compare your program to what you're doing now (your ministry assignments, relationships, and degree program). Show this comparison to someone who's completed seminary and been in ministry for several years and get his or her input.

Adjust your life accordingly.

5
Live Off Campus

Seminary housing can be more affordable than comparable accommodations in surrounding communities. It is definitely more convenient.

There is a drawback associated with on-campus living, however. Seminary is not the real world. It is a bubble, insulated both physically and culturally from the lost community around it. In one sense, this is good. Seminary should be a place you can saturate yourself in the biblical worldview and Christian community. The word seminary means "seed-bed." It's an incubator—a safe place for Christian leaders to grow.

But the safety of seminary also makes it cozy. It's very easy to get comfortable living in a place where everyone shares the same basic convictions and worldview. It's easy to get used to living without regular contact with non-Christians.

The life of a seminary student is pretty culturally insulated. You go to school with Christians, you read only Christian books (who has time to read anything else?), and you serve in a local Christian church. In short, you're surrounded by Christians! The only place you might have to interact with unbelievers where you work, but many seminary students end up working for churches, Christian ministries, or in Christian companies. In the end, many seminary students have little or no contact, friendship, or ministry opportunities with lost people.

See how easy it can be to completely lose touch with the people we need to reach?

If it only takes three to six weeks to form a habit, what will three to four years of living an insulated life in the seminary bubble do to you?

Many pastors and Christian leaders leave the insulation of seminary, and go straight into church work where the habit naturally continues. When Christian leaders do not engage with lost people, most times their churches will not, either. Insulated leaders make for an insulated church that does not share the gospel.

Live off-campus so you can escape the Christian ghetto. Wherever you live, you need a plan to engage regularly with the real, lost people around you.

If you choose to live on campus, ask yourself this: how am I getting out of the seminary bubble into the real world?

6
Avoid the "Seminary Church"

Particularly around larger seminaries, you'll find what I call the "seminary church." It's almost always a large church. Often, it's close to the campus. Many professors and students attend it. The culture and theology of the seminary often bleeds over into the church. For seminary students, it's a comfy place to be.

There were a few churches like this at my seminary. One of them had so many seminary students, they had multiple Sunday school classes just for those students. I can't imagine a greater waste of giftedness and potential. Groups of twelve to twenty men and women preparing for ministry sat in a class on Sunday mornings expecting someone from that church to lead and teach them. It was basically a repeat of what they had done all week in class!

Don't do that. God did not call you to ministry so you can sit and be served. Every seminary student should serve on Sundays. There are dozens of churches within driving distance of your seminary that desperately need leaders. Go to those churches, assume some responsibilities, and make a difference.

Some of you will have the opportunity to serve as full-time or part-time pastors or staff ministers of a church while studying at seminary. You'll be underpaid and overworked, but it is probably the best ministry preparation you can find.

Even if don't find a paid position, find a church where you can have responsibility for leading some kind of ministry: youth, children, senior adults, or discipleship. Teach a Sunday School class. Lead the outreach ministry. Coordinate Children's Church. Preach at a nursing home. Help your pastor with sermon research or hospital visitation. The opportunities are abundant and will help prepare you for future ministry.

There *are* a handful of "seminary churches" that deliberately and strategically invest in seminary students by training them to lead and preparing them for ministry. If you happen to find this kind of opportunity for mentoring and development, then by all means, embrace it.

A few suggestions:

Pray for God's leadership. God uses our current tasks to prepare us for our next assignments, so choose prayerfully.

Ask around. Some students may be serving in a less-known church with plenty of needs. Seminary placement offices often have information about local churches with full- or part-time ministry positions.

Don't be picky. We all know churches aren't perfect, so don't expect it. The preaching may be average, the music may be crummy, and the people may be weird. Get used to it.

Look for a pastor to learn from. If you're not pastoring a church yourself, then look carefully at the pastor when you consider a church. They won't be good at everything—no pastor is—but they will have some strengths you can learn from, either through up close mentoring or your intentional observation from afar.

Find a church quickly. Don't spend months and months in the search. Consider a few, then decide, join, and settle. I'd suggest that you join a church by mid-term of your first semester.

Volunteer. Go straight to your pastor and find out where and how you can serve. Start serving as soon as possible.

Support your pastor. You'll probably find things about your pastor's leadership you disagree with. As a general rule, you should support him, unless his theology is clearly heretical, in which case you should leave. Don't murmur against him or join an insurrection. It won't be long before you're the flawed leader who needs support.

Plan to stay. Church hopping, by leaders and members, is epidemic. It's a sign of immaturity. Staying in one place will teach you lessons that hopping around won't. By staying in one place over time you will more effectively learn to love people, manage conflict, navigate church politics, and lead change. Join a church and stay there.

MANAGE YOUR TIME

7
Seminary Survival Skill # 1: Triage

Write this down and put it on your bathroom mirror: You can't do everything.

Seminary life comes with multiple demands, all of which are too much for any one person. There's no way for you to work the hours to get all the money you need and make straight "A"s in school, maintain an intimate walk with God, pour yourself out in fruitful ministry, develop an impressive resume, see to the needs of your spouse and family, develop a network of friendships to support you, and get the rest, exercise, and proper nutrition you need.

It's just not possible. These endeavors require more time and energy than any one person has. So please give up the illusion of doing everything at 100%. If you are a perfectionist, read the last paragraph again.

To survive, you must learn how and when to say *no*. There will be some things in your life that simply will not get the attention they need. The earlier you reconcile yourself to that fact, the better off you'll be.

Learning to Say Yes, No, and Wait.

Ever been to an emergency room on a Friday night? The waiting area holds a throng of injured, sometimes bleeding, people. Why do they have to wait? Can't they get any help?

Let me introduce you to the idea of triage.

> Triage (`tree-ahzh), from French, "to sort."
>
> 1. A process for sorting injured people into groups based on their need for or likely benefit from immediate medical treatment. Triage is used in hospital emergency rooms, on battlefields, and at disaster sites when limited medical resources must be allocated.
>
> 2. A system used to allocate a scarce commodity, such as food, only to those capable of deriving the greatest benefit from it.
>
> 3. A process in which things are ranked in terms of importance or priority.[i]

If you are injured and go to an emergency room, your first stop will be to see the triage nurse. He or she will quickly evaluate you, decide how urgent your condition is, and determine when you will be seen. If you are about to die, you'll probably be seen immediately. If your injuries are not life-threatening, however, be prepared to wait. It's not unusual for some people to wait in the emergency room for hours, while others are whisked back and seen in minutes. It's not a fair system at all.

Compare this to a customer service call center. While you're on hold, the recorded message tells you that "your call will be answered in the order in which it was received." There's a line. The next person in line gets served. It's fair. Everyone gets treated equally.

The triage nurse is not popular with people in the waiting room. But it is his or her job to see that the hospital's resources are maximized so that lives are saved. If emergency rooms were like customer service centers—first-come, first-served—then people would die of heart attacks in the waiting room as doctors gave their attention to relatively minor cuts and scrapes that arrived first.

Seminary life is like an emergency room, not a customer service center. You cannot play fair with time, tasks, and relationships. You must learn to sort them according to their importance and priority. Some items you need to ignore, others you need to let wait, and others should get your immediate attention. Triage requires vision and toughness. It requires a clear understanding of your goals and the big picture. It requires a determination to make the hard choices that will get you there.

Triage isn't just for seminary. Once you graduate, you'll find that life in ministry is the same. There are always more people to see and things to do than you have time for.

You must be able to say no.

Saying no is not easy for anyone, least of all seminary students, who go into ministry because they like helping people. To test your own fortitude, try this exercise: take a day or two and say no every time someone asks you to do something.

> "Can you help me bring in this box?" No.

> "Do you have a second?" No.

> "We're having a party and…" No.

It's not easy. It requires guts. But to survive ministry, you need be able to say no.

People will ask you to do all kinds of things. If you are too quick with your "yes," you will bog down in unimportant minutiae that can steer your whole life off mission (I'm convinced that many churches lose focus because their leaders say yes to good things at the expense of the most important.). You must defend your borders.

Practice saying no. Remember, you're not doing it to be a jerk; you're doing it so you can say yes to the important things.

The Polite Way to Say No

Caroline Webb recommends this approach to declining invitations:

First, warmly thank the person for the invitation.

> "I'm so honored that you thought of me! Very kind of you."

Next, positively inform them about the reason you have to say no.

> "You know, one of the things I'm really excited about is my Family Reunion coming up next week. I'm going to get to see some people I haven't seen in a long time."

Finally, say no.

> "And since I have to work ahead for when I'm going to be gone next week, I'm afraid I'm not going to be able to [teach the class, attend the party, etc.]"

Putting the reason before the no takes some of the sting out of declining.[ii]

Still Can't Say No? Try the "Qualified Yes"

If you struggle with saying no outright, here's a more polite option: the "qualified yes." It's basically a yes with defined limits.

> Can you lead our Bible study every Thursday night? You'd be great.

Instead of yes, try, "Yes, I can help you for the first four weeks. After that, I could do once a month."

> Can you proofread my paper? "Yes, if you email it to me by 4:00 today."

> Can you lead VBS for 3rd graders this year? "Yes, if you can find me an assistant and manage on Thursday when I'm gone."

> Can you come to our class reunion? "Yes, if it's not in June."

Can we talk? "Yes, I can give you 15 minutes."

Can you drop what you're doing and help me on this project? "Yes, if you extend my deadlines on these other three projects."

By introducing the qualification on the front end, you're protecting your time. It's not as strong as a flat-out no, but it's better than an unqualified yes.

Remember, time is a currency. In seminary, it might be the most valuable currency you have. Handing over your time indiscriminately is like handing over your money to anyone who asks.

To survive seminary, and to survive in ministry, you must learn triage.

8
Map Out Your Degree

Now that you're enrolled in seminary, get a copy of your degree program—the list of all the classes you need to take to graduate.

Choose a priority.

Don't try to be good at everything. Think about the pastors and Christian leaders you know. Usually, they are really good at one or two things. It's a function of their personality, spiritual gifts, talents and preparation. The goal of being "well-rounded," i.e. competent at a lot of things, is good for when you are young and don't yet know what you're good at. By now, however, you should have a grasp of what your emerging gifts and strengths are. In seminary, you should aim to capitalize on that.

So, within your curriculum plan, choose a focus for yourself that aligns with your strengths and interests. Are you a good critical thinker, or do you want to be? You might pay attention to systematic theology, ethics, or philosophy of religion. Are you a people person? Focus on evangelism and pastoral care. Are you a strong communicator? Focus on preaching. A gifted teacher? Old and New Testament or maybe Greek and Hebrew. A great organizer? Education administration. You get the idea.

The first reason for choosing a focus is that if you have the freedom to choose your electives, you can choose the ones that will reinforce your objective. Second, when time and life pressures come to bear and some of your classwork has to give, you know the areas you are committed to giving 100%, and which are a lower priority.

Since you're new to the seminary world, be prepared for a few surprises. You may find, unexpectedly, that you love or despise one subject or another. Still, you should start with an idea of what you really want to take away from seminary. Feel free to revise your plan as you go.

Rank your classes by difficulty.

Some classes are going to be harder, and some will be easier. If you're not sure, ask your fellow students. They know. Greek and Hebrew will be difficult and time intensive. Classes in Pastoral Ministry or Missions, probably not so much. Some of the difficulty level depends on the subject matter and some depends on which professor you take. Consult students who are a year or two ahead of you as you develop your schedule.

Color-code them. Use red, yellow, and green for hard, moderate and fair course difficulty.

Make a semester-by-semester plan

You might only be able to map out one or two semesters ahead, and you will certainly have to modify it as you go. Some classes may fill up and not be available when you want to take them. Projecting a plan like this, however, will help in a number of ways. A plan will enable you to read ahead for coming semesters if you are able. You can use your plan to make sure you don't take too many difficult classes at the same time. Most of all, it will give you a big picture of your entire seminary experience. When you get tired halfway through your program, one glance at it can encourage you with your current progress and reassure you that the end is coming!

Most of all, it will help you keep your eyes on the big picture as pressures mount. You won't be able to give your best effort to every moment in seminary, but you don't have to. Some of your classes will have to suffer so that you can give attention to your family, or to classes that are more important to you, or to other things. A degree plan will help you exercise triage intelligently instead of randomly.

Questions to consider:

What are my one or two best strengths as a minister? What do I see in myself, and what do others see in me?

Which core classes and/or electives are going to best build on those strengths?

What one thing in my curriculum do I want to become an expert on?

Extras:

Go to seminarysurvivalguide.com/book-extras for extra resources, including sample degree planning tools you can download and customize.

9
Syllabus Strategies for a Successful Semester

The first week of seminary is a fantastic gift. By the beginning of each class, if not before, they provide a syllabus, which contains all the assignments you'll need to complete this semester and their due dates.

The class syllabus is a time management bonanza. If you take a few moments to plan well, it can make the semester much easier for you.

Here's what you need to do:

Calendar Everything

1. Get your calendar. You should have only one calendar, because you have only one life. Be sure you coordinate well with your spouse and kids.

2. Note all the dates of your papers and exams.

3. To the best of your ability, block out study and writing time in the week before each exam. Block out study time two weeks before each paper is due.

4. Schedule recovery time. Be sure to schedule some down time right after mid-terms, and after big assignments are due. Plan to relax a bit. If you schedule a day trip, a date, or some fun activity just after the crunch, it will give you something to look forward to after the big project.

5. Make a note of when the worst crunch times are, like midterms and finals. If you're married, discuss it with your spouse. If your job allows for any scheduling leeway, let your boss know early. If you're a valuable employee, she just might work with you.

Following these suggestions will save you time and frustration all semester long.

Start Reading Now

Seminary involves a LOT of reading. At the beginning of the semester, you typically have more open time. Seize it! Use it to read ahead now, and then when the first wave of papers is due, you won't be so rushed.

There may be some classes where you can read ahead more easily.

Look over your assigned reading, and decide which reading will be more challenging and which is more accessible. You may want to wade through the difficult stuff early, or breeze through the easy stuff first. Either way, get a jump on it.

One friend of mine who is in seminary now reads ahead an entire semester. He gets the syllabi for the coming semester, and does all his reading before the semester starts. Then during the current semester, he reads for the following semester.

Check out the chapter "Master Your Seminary's Required Reading" to save you even more time.

Even if you can only get an extra six hours or so of reading in during the first few weeks, that will give you six hours you can use later when it's crunch time.

Craft a Writing Plan for Every Major Paper

Writing papers on the scale that seminary requires can be daunting if you haven't done it before. Ten to fifteen page papers are common; so are twenty-five to thirty page papers. Most undergraduate work doesn't require writing of this length.

It will help you if you create a writing plan for each major paper. Here's how.

First, Break It Down

To create a writing plan, begin by breaking down the project into manageable tasks. Make a list of everything you'll need to do:

- Assess topic choices.
- Choose a topic. Choose a topic that interests you or will strengthen your future ministry.
- Get topic approved by your professor.

- Find sources.
- Research your sources and take notes on them.
- Formulate a thesis.
- Create an outline.
- Write a first draft.
- Revise your paper and write a final draft.
- Format the paper.
- Proofread.
- Make final corrections and submit.

The level of detail you choose is partly a function of how you think about the project, and how big the assignment is.

Second, Estimate the Time

Estimate how much actual clock time will be needed for each task in the breakdown, and write it down. For instance,

- Assess topic choices (10 minutes)
- Choose a topic (1 minute)
- Get topic approved by your professor (5 minutes)
- Find sources (3 hours)
- Research your sources and take notes on them. (6 hours)
- Formulate a thesis (10 minutes)
- Create an outline (20 minutes)
- Write first draft (4-6 hours)
- Revise, and write final draft. (3 hours)
- Proofread. (30 minutes)

Your time estimates will vary depending on the size of each project and the pace at which you work. Pay attention to your time estimates; they will often be way off. Make note of how long each step actually takes, so you'll be able to make more precise plans for future projects.

Third, Reserve the Time Now

Finally, this step is important, block off time in your calendar for each task, beginning anywhere from one to four weeks before the due date. I'd suggest that you plan to finish at least a couple of days before the due date to give you some leeway if you fall behind schedule.

If possible, start the paper early. In some classes, you have to cover a certain amount of material before you're prepared to write some papers, but not always.

Make A Study Plan for Each Major Exam

Similar to creating a writing plan for papers, you should block out dedicated study time for major exams.

If you do this now, at the beginning of the semester (and stick to your schedule), then you won't be pinched to find time to study.

It's pretty simple:

- Reserve study blocks beginning about a week before the exam.
- Plan for multiple, short study times rather than longer blocks. Four 30-minute blocks will probably make for better retention than a single two-hour marathon review.
- Reserve this time now, and plan around it.

Also consider these study ideas:

- Swap class notes with someone and read over your friend's notes. This will help refresh your memory of lectures and pick up things you might have missed.
- If you've underlined and/or highlighted your class reading well, it should be relatively easy to review what you've read.
- Get a friend to quiz you on points you'll be tested on. Iron sharpens iron, and it's a good excuse to get coffee.

10

Planning Your Week: The Time Map

The week is the basic organizational unit of the semester. Classes during the week, regular work or ministry hours, and church on Sunday form the basic rhythm for a seminary student each semester.

One strong way to strategically manage your week is to use a Time Map. A time map resembles a weekly appointment calendar, but instead of recording specific activities, a time map establishes zones for when you are going to do what type of activity, based upon your goals and priorities.

Take a look at the blank time map on the next page. (We have a blank, downloadable time map on the book extras page on the website.)

	Sunday	Monday	Tuesday	Wednesday
6:00 AM				
7:00 AM				
8:00 AM				
9:00 AM				
10:00 AM				
11:00 AM				
12:00 PM				
1:00 PM				
2:00 PM				
3:00 PM				

To get started, write down what you will do each week, thinking in terms of categories. Here's a sample list to get you started:

- Classes
- Study
- Work (Job 1: Starbucks)
- Work (Job 2: Library)

- Prayer time
- Gym/exercise time
- Spouse/Social/Family time
- Ministry
- Church
- Rest
- Wake up / get ready
- Wind down / go to bed

Many of these times are set already for you. Your class times, possibly your work hours, church on Sundays, etc. Fill these in.

Then, think strategically through the rest. When will you study? Consider: are you best in the morning or at night? If you have the freedom to (you might not), put your study time when you're mentally the sharpest. When will you spend family time? Set a regular time for it, ideally one that does not change from week to week.

When will you rise and when will you go to bed? I'm personally a morning person who is most productive before 11:00am, so getting up early and going to bed early allows me to be the most productive. My brain slumps after lunch, so afternoon is best for the gym, for meetings with people, etc. Be aware of your own rhythms and, to the degree that you can, plan activities during the times of day that are best for them.

Fill in the rest of your time map with the kind of activity you will do. For instance, prayer and workout early, class in the morning, study after lunch, work mid-afternoon to close.

Depending on your personality, you may want a more rigid and specific time map, or one that's more general and loose. Either way can work just fine.

Here's part of a sample time map, just to give you the idea.

	Sunday	Monday	Tuesday	Wednesday
6:00 AM		Wake, pray, shower		
7:00 AM		Commute		
8:00 AM	Church			
9:00 AM			Classes	
10:00 AM				
11:00 AM				
12:00 PM		Lunch		
1:00 PM	Work	Gym		
2:00 PM			Study	
3:00 PM				

The point of it is to make sure that you have time dedicated to each activity and relationship. If you fill up your time map and realize you don't have any room for study, or work, or your family, then re-work it until you are satisfied with it.

Time is a limited but equally distributed resource: everyone gets 168 hours a week, and we all spend it doing something. A Time Map will help you use yours judiciously.

Extras:

Go to <u>seminarysurvivalguide.com/book-extras</u> for extra resources, including sample time maps and book recommendations.

II

Tips for a Productive Day at Seminary

Here's a baker's dozen of my favorite tips for daily productivity.

Get up early. Sleeping in is fun, but should be an occasional treat. Jesus' example of early rising is worthy of imitation.

Eat breakfast. Kick start the metabolism. Cereal and fruit is easy and nutritious.

Spend time with God first. Get your spirit in a place of peace and adoration before you tackle the day.

Plan your day. Grab your calendar, and preview the day: classes, work schedule, appointments, etc. Don't forget about long term projects that you need to be working on. Read ahead for classes if you can.

Make a quick to-do list of things you want to get done that day.

Prioritize. Choose two or three items that are the most important for you to get done that day. No more than three!!

Hit it early. Try to accomplish either your most important task or your most dreaded task before 11:00am.

Utilize down time. If you have a spare ten minutes in your day, go to your to-do list, and find items that will take 2 minutes or less to do, and plow through a few (pay bills, make a phone call, return an email, etc.).

Make time for relationships. Life is not fundamentally about tasks; it's about relationships. One of the reasons we want to organize our days productively is so we can dispatch tasks and have time for relationships. Whether it's coffee or phone call with a friend, a walk with your spouse, or playing with your kids, a productive day includes relationship time. Don't let the urgent crowd out the important!

Beware of time wasters. Limit your media consumption and avoid unplanned, open-ended social hangout time.

Set yourself up for success tomorrow morning. Set out your coffee mug, make your lunch, lay out clothes, organize your school bag, tidy up a bit... a few minutes of prep tonight can make for a smooth launch in the morning.

Wind down. Leave some time to wind down at the end of the day--with a book, your spouse, or in prayer.

Go to bed. "He grants sleep to those He loves" (Psalm 127:2, NIV). Avoid the lure of glowing screen time (TV, computer, cell phone), which can keep you up too late and rob you of needed sleep. Be done with all that early in the evening, and get to bed on time, if not early.

Extras:

Go to seminarysurvivalguide.com/book-extras for extra resources, including Leo Babauta's wonderful article "How to Become an Early Riser."

12

Master Your Seminary's Required Reading in Half the Time (or Less)

Seminary requires a massive amount of reading. Often the workload for even a single course can go over a thousand pages. Multiply that by four or five, and it becomes daunting, especially if you're not a natural reader. The number of people who struggle with reading seems to be growing, and I'm sure that's the case in seminary, also.

Unfortunately, some of your assigned books will be a waste of your time. I still remember when my education principles professor, a well-respected scholar, held up a blue and silver book on the first day of class and chirped, "This is an excellent book." Liar. It was 300 pages of absolutely useless abstraction and gobbledygook.

So, as you're assembling your massive stack of books for the coming semester, I want to share an approach to reading that should save you some time and help you learn more. This approach is not unique; it is standard fare for graduate students.

By the way, your professors may disagree with this advice.

Never read a book from cover to cover (unless you really want to).

The Pareto Principle, applied to reading, teaches that 80% of the value of a book can be found in 20% of its pages. That means that reading all of a book will be a low-value use of your time, your professor's insistence to the contrary notwithstanding. So unless you really want to, don't read any book from cover to cover. Try this instead:[iii]

Read the introduction and opening chapter to get the general thesis of the book.

Then skip to the end, and survey the author's conclusions. Once you have a feel for the main theme, go back to the table of contents, and look for where the most valuable content should be. Often, an author takes a few chapters to establish background for his main point—these chapters can be skimmed or even skipped entirely. Look for what appear to be the most relevant chapters, and give your attention there.

To read a chapter: read the opening paragraph or two, then the closing paragraph or two. Then scan through the headings, if the book has them. If the book has no headings, read the opening sentence of every paragraph instead. You can dip in and read the full text anywhere that the content seems rich or relevant. Feel free to skip around if you want.

One caution: some books cannot be read profitably this way. Greek and Hebrew grammars, for instance, cannot be skimmed, nor can closely argued philosophy or theology texts. You can, however, get through most standard textbooks more quickly with this method.

Read with a pencil.

Reading, done well, is not a passive activity. It should be interactive. You should be thinking actively about the content, and challenging and asking questions of the author as you go.

To do this, read with a pencil (or pen, highlighter, etc.). Underline key phrases and main points as you go. If a question occurs to you, write it in the margins. Recognize an idea from another class or book? Make a note of it. This will help you when you come back to review later.

Why does this work? Underlining requires you to think about the material and make a definite choice about what is most significant. Writing in the margin forces you to express that vague objection to the author's idea in specific words. Writing encourages clarity and specificity.

Some people have a deep reverence toward their books, and feel that writing in them is a sacrilege. Get over it. Your books are not there for you to worship and preserve; they are there to help you learn. You're a student, not a librarian.

Discuss the reading with other students.

Discussing what you've (mostly) read with other readers will help confirm and enrich your grasp of the material. You might even compare your understanding of the reading with others who slogged through the whole thing, and see how much (if anything) you're missing.

Re-read.

Since you're not slogging through the entire text, you can use some of the time you save to come back to the text, and re-read. This will help when reviewing for exams. Or, if you're not satisfied that you've gotten everything you need, then you can come back to sections that you skimmed earlier and read more closely.

Audio Books

For some books, getting the audio version is a win: you can "read" them during your commuting or exercise time. I did this with some of my PhD seminars: I bought the audio version of one or two of my 12-15 books in each seminar, and listened to them while I walked my dog. I found that audio worked best with historical or narrative books. More technical books, which I would need to pore over more closely or refer back to often, were best in print. One memorable audio book was *God Is Not Great* by Christopher Hitchens. The author read it himself, and his disdainful, arrogant tone dripped from every sentence. Very entertaining.

Ebooks

Consider electronic versions, too: I have an older Kindle that will read books to me (if that feature is not disabled by the publisher). Kindle books have searchable text, which is very handy. Not all ebooks retain the page numbers of the print editions, however, so if you need to cite it, you might have to get the print version or learn the appropriate way to cite electronic versions of a book at your seminary.

Objections

"I paid a month's salary for these books! I'm reading all of them! I have to get my money's worth!"

That's fine. Read all of them. But remember you bought those books to serve you and help you learn. If you insist on reading every word, you may find that you become a servant to your books, rather than the other way around.

"My professor requires me to sign off on having read every word of every book."

On the website, we had a spirited discussion of this practice of some professors. I will spare you my diatribe on ill-advised pedagogy. Some professors do this because they think (not incorrectly) that some students are lazy and want to do the least they can to get by.

Reading books the way I'm recommending is not easier, but it is more efficient. In some ways, I think it's actually more difficult than reading straight through. When you're dissecting a book this way, you have to be actively thinking about what the author is saying and what you are learning. At the end of the day, do as you will: if your professor asks this question, answer with integrity. But don't think that having your eyes touch every word of a book is somehow a better way of reading. Depending on the book, and on your knowledge of the subject, it may not be.

The final caveat: a well-known seminary professor once told me that Masters-level students do not yet have the discernment to be able to tell which parts of a book are more valuable. I actually agree with him. For many of your classes, it will be your first exposure to the subject matter, its concepts and categories. However, I think that the purpose of education is to make you such a discerner. You have to begin practicing your discernment skills sometime. Might as well start now.

More importantly, your professor doesn't have to manage the competing demands upon your time. You do.

Not convinced? Try this approach with just one class, and see if it helps you.

Extras:

Go to seminarysurvivalguide.com/book-extras for extra resources, including our rapid reading tools infographic.

13
No One Cares What Your Grades Are

I've always been a grade-nerd. I was in the gifted program from 3rd grade through high school. Once I discovered that I had academic gifts, I found I liked making "A"s. My parents never settled for less. In high school, when I brought home six "A"s and one "B" on the report card, my parents' terse response was, "Bring it up."

In seminary, I approached it the same way. I had to make "A"s. HAD to. Some of you are just like me.

Here's the reality check: No one cares what your grades are in seminary.

Unless you want to do doctoral work, your grades should not be something you are overly concerned about. I was always concerned about my grades, so I worked hard and did well in seminary. My M.Div. GPA was 4.018 on a 4.0 scale.

Do you know how many people have asked me what my grades were in seminary? Not one. A big, fat zero.

Churches don't care. When you interview for a ministry position, your 4.0 M.Div., sadly, will be worth the same to them as your buddy's 2.8 M.Div.

Your peers don't care. Your congregation doesn't care. Your denomination doesn't care. And, to top it off, your seminary does not care.

This was the worst insult to my grade-nerdness. For my stellar grade-making performance, my seminary gave me exactly nothing. No pat on the back. No form letter from the dean, no sticker on my diploma, no gold sash at graduation. Nothing.

So to all you grade-nerds out there: loosen your collar and relax. You are not a grade on a page.

The fantastic side of this is that not having to make straight "A"s gives you a bit of latitude. Instead of giving extra hours to that paper in that low value class (trust me, you'll know which ones they are) you can spend time in ministry, or on a job project, or with your family. Making a "C" in Education Administration (zzzzz) is probably not the worst choice you can make.

Here's another reason to give up being a grade nerd: Grading is a system that rewards not only academic performance, but also compliance. It rewards those who follow all the rules and do what they are told. It might be controversial to suggest this, but the best church leaders may not be the ones who are the best at following established conventions. I daresay a pastor who complies with every expectation of the old guard at his church will likely lead a dwindling congregation. Brave ministry leadership will almost always require bucking conventional expectations. Working had to make straight-"A"s may reflect stellar academic performance, but on another level, it trains you to be an obedient conformist.

But You Should

No one else may care what your grades are in seminary, but you should.

You *should* care about your grades, to the degree that they reflect your stewardship of your education. The opportunity you have for a seminary education is a rare gift that many thousands of pastors all over the world would give their right arm for, if they even had the chance.

Can you stand with clean conscience before God about the effort you're putting into your seminary coursework?

If you're one of those students who want to get by with the minimum, who hang back and don't exert or stretch yourself at all, then why are you even there? If you wanted an "easier" education, then spend $200 on popular level Christian living books. It'll be easier, cheaper, and you won't have to think.

If you're preparing to lead God's people, however, you'd better prepare well and work hard.

A dean of students at a leading evangelical seminary told me that one of the two major problems he found with students was their glaring lack of industry.

I remember these students, especially in my Philosophy of Religion class. Our professor required us to read and think at higher levels than we ever had before, and it was very hard. Some of the guys in my class really resented it and whined in class about how hard the assignments were.

Go to the ant, O sluggard. Study to show yourself approved. You should work hard.

Now, sometimes, even if you work hard, your grades won't be that great. And that's ok. The key question is the heart question: have you worked diligently and wisely?

MANAGE YOUR MONEY

14

Learn How Money Works

There is more information on personal finance available now than ever before. Scores of books have been written on it, not to mention the hundreds of websites and blogs that dot the electric landscape, covering every imaginable topic: budgeting, loans, debt management, mortgages, retirement savings, and much more. In the Christian world, Dave Ramsey, Larry Burkett, and Ron Blue have devoted their lives to helping people manage their money and achieve financial freedom.

And yet, most people are financially illiterate. Few schools teach money management, so unless your family taught you how to handle money, you may not know the difference between a stock and a bond, APR and APY, or simple versus compound interest.

Economist Richard Thaler comments that the modern economy is so complex that even ordinary decisions like buying a car or taking out a student loan can be hard to get right even for graduate students in economics. "Throwing the financially illiterate into that maelstrom," he writes, "is like taking students currently enrolled in driver's education and asking them to compete in the Indianapolis 500."[iv]

Every seminary student needs to learn how money works.

Get Educated

One critical difference between ordinary people and wealthy people is the wealthy know how to manage their money. They learned to track where every dollar goes, how to budget their money, how to live off less than they make, to invest early in life, and how to stay out of debt.

These principles, if you obey them, will enable you to graduate seminary debt free. They are the principles that will empower you to give generously and allow you to serve your church wholeheartedly without the fear of making ends meet at the end of the month.

Be honest: how much do you really know about personal finance? If the answer is "not much," well, you're not alone. The good news is that you can fill in the gaps and self-educate in this area quite easily. There are some suggestions below on how to get started.

Information alone, of course, is not enough. If it were, everyone would be billionaires and have six pack abs. Information is a beginning. Experience adds to and deepens our understanding, but the genius factor most people are missing is financial coaching.

Find a Financial Coach

Over the past few decades, Tiger Woods has consistently been ranked one of the top athletes in the world over a range of measures, including salary, physical capabilities, and performance. In addition, however, there also has been constant buzz about who is coaching Tiger. When Hank Haney stopped coaching him and David Ledbetter took over, sports media reported it as headline news. Tiger, the best golfer in the world, sought advice constantly. He'd even change where he was getting advice if he didn't think it was helping anymore.

If you want to be the best money manager you can be, seek wisdom in a coach or financial mentor.

The wealthiest people in the world constantly seek out professional help with managing their money. They keep up with the markets, they discuss current events that affect their investments, and they continually look for more opportunities to earn and invest.

A pastor friend of mine loves telling the story about moving back home from college and finding out that Larry Burkett lived just a few houses down from him in North Georgia. You better believe he took advantage of that wisdom and sought counsel from him as frequently as possible. Find someone you can trust to give you real advice and help you along your journey.

If we seek wise counsel before we get married, and in our spiritual walk, why wouldn't we seek the help and insight of a mentor in something as important as our finances?

Take the First Step

Whether your first step is to start eliminating current debt, making your first investment for retirement, reading a good book on personal finance, or just laying out a budget for your family, you *have* to take the first step. You must begin the journey. Pray for wisdom and success in this endeavor and watch how God uses your finances to become a blessing and not a burden.

Here are some suggestions:

- Read a book on personal finance. The book extras page has links to some suggested titles.
- Start following a blog or podcast on personal finance.
- Find someone who is a successful money manager and have coffee with them. There are probably some people who are good with money at your church. Ask around.
- Start a personal financial inventory by answering these questions: what do I earn, what do I spend, how much do I owe, and what do I own?
- Sit down and hammer out a budget.

Whatever it is, do it. Inspiration is great, but action is better.

Extras:

Go to seminarysurvivalguide.com/book-extras for extra resources, including book and blog recommendations.

15
How to Graduate Debt Free

Two Chairs

"When I was a boy, my father introduced me to the wonders of song," tenor Luciano Pavarotti relates. "He urged me to work very hard to develop my voice. Arrigo Pola, a professional tenor in my hometown of Modena, Italy, took me as a pupil. I also enrolled in a teachers' college. On graduating, I asked my father, 'Shall I be a teacher or a singer?'

"'Luciano,' my father replied, 'if you try to sit on two chairs, you will fall between them. For life, you must choose one chair.'

"I chose one. And now I think whether it's laying bricks, writing a book—whatever we choose—we should give ourselves to it. Commitment, that's the key. Choose one chair."[v]

In our finances, we get to choose between two chairs. The first chair is financial freedom; the second is the anchoring shackle of debt. Becoming debt free, for most, seems like an impossible task. There are, however, many people that manage live 100% debt free. They have zero credit card bills, car notes, school loans, or mortgages.

The costs associated with a life of debt are enormous. Struggling to pay bills at the end of the month, working a job you don't love, and never having enough to cover expenses can be draining and exhausting. Living debt free isn't easy either, but you can do it. You can become debt free. Remember: commitment is key. Choose the right chair.

You do not need to go into debt to graduate with a seminary education.

One misconception about seminary is that it's permanently tied to a mountain of debt. This does not need to be the case. There are ways to graduate debt free. Below are a few important decisions that can help make this a reality in your future.

1. **Start your journey debt free**. You are in the driver's seat of your journey to financial freedom. Ultimately *you* are the one who will make your financial decisions. It's far, far easier to graduate debt free if you start out debt free.

   Use the Domino Effect to eliminate debt: Determine your smallest debt and lock your sights on it. Put all of your energy into knocking out that smallest debt first. Once that debt is eliminated, rollover those funds to your second smallest debt. Repeat this process until you are targeting serious amounts of money at your larger debts. Rid yourself of all credit card debt and student loans *before* you start seminary.

Adding new debt to existing debt is *not* a path to freedom.

2. **Test Drive**. Try ministry before you start seminary. Experience in ministry is invaluable. It not only makes you a more attractive candidate for future positions, but, more importantly, it will help you determine if ministry really is what you want to do with your life. Ministry is not for everybody. If you figure that out before you start seminary or even early in the process, you could save over $50,000 in expenditures. According to Daryl Eldridge, founder of Rockbridge Seminary, fifty percent of seminary graduates are no longer in vocational ministry five years after graduation. [vi] Be sure about ministry before you start seminary.

3. **Pay as you go**. It's better to extend your schooling over several years and pay as you go than to spend the next 15 to 20 years paying off a loan.

4. **Consider the cost**. The landscape of education has changed. Students are no longer restricted to residential, brick and mortar seminaries. There are now distance and online options that can save you, either in tuition or in relocation cost and living expenses. Does it make financial sense to be on campus when you can save money by taking the class remotely? You might be able to procure a better paying job if you stay in your area rather than relocating for residential seminary. Some churches are now beginning to offer church-based ministry training in partnership with seminaries. If it's an option, investigate it. It could save you serious money.

5. **Apply for scholarships**. While scarce, scholarships are out there. Look for school specific scholarships as you begin and also scholarships that become available after you finish a term or two.

6. **Ask for help**. Inquire if your church has seminary funding or continuing education options. If you're on staff at a church, there's a good chance your church may offer funding for further education.

Reality Check

Of all the degreed professionals in America, the two lowest paid professions, in order, are pastor and teacher.[vii]

- A pastor of a church of **50-100** can expect to make **$46,278.25**
- A pastor of a church of **100-200** can expect to make $50,294.96
- A pastor of a church of **200-500** can expect to make $59,244.31
- A pastor of a church of **500-1000** can expect to make $72,359.61[viii]

Seminary creates enough of its own stress; don't add to it by piling on debt. Refuse to fall into the temptation that you have to go into debt to get through school. Consider the effects this debt will have on your lifestyle, family, and giving as you come out of school. It will take years to pay back a huge debt when you are living on a minister's salary.

"The rich rule over the poor, and the borrower is slave to the lender." (Proverbs 22:7, ESV)

Extras:

Go to <u>seminarysurvivalguide.com/book-extras</u> for book recommendations and other resources.

16

Manage Your Money Wisely

Most ministry careers don't come with high incomes. Mastering the basic principles of money management, therefore, is more critical for seminary students than for many others. Additionally, as a leader in the church, you will want to begin setting an example now.

The following, time-tested, proven principles will help you find a balanced approach to financial freedom.

Avoid Extremes

The most obvious extreme to avoid is living beyond your means. It is a reckless habit. There are plenty of companies that will encourage you to live a lifestyle that you cannot afford. They will sell you cars, furniture, electronics, and clothes on credit and help you live like a millionaire right now if you want. They also will shackle you with a burden of debt you might carry for decades.

If you're in seminary, however, it is likely that to a large degree you have left behind the typical American dream of success: nice cars, big houses, and keeping up with the Joneses. I say "to a large degree" because no matter how self-denying or ministry-focused we are, we are all surrounded by a consumer culture that affects us in ways that are not always obvious.

A second extreme to avoid is that of financial legalism, where every penny is pinched, self-denial is the only mindset, and there is no room for even small indulgences. A friend told me about a man who so tightly controlled his family's finances that if his wife bought a candy bar, he expected her to turn in a receipt. There comes a point where relentless financial restriction becomes a stress-inducing burden. Be frugal, but sensible.

Live on Less

It's easy to think earning more money is the fastest way to solve your financial problems. Increasing your income is a key element of financial prosperity (which will be addressed in the next chapter), but it is not a fix all—especially if your spending habits are out of control.

What many people fail to understand is that reducing expenses is actually a faster way to get more money. Consider: if you get a $1000/year raise, you don't actually get another $1000 to spend. You must first pay income tax on that raise, which, depending on your marginal tax rate, could be a significant chunk. If your marginal rate is 25% (not uncommon), that $1000 raise means only $750 in extra money.

By contrast, every dollar you save on expenses is all yours — to keep or to spend. Thus the saying, "a penny saved is a penny earned."

Thomas Stanley's best-selling book *The Millionaire Next Door* told the story of people with modest incomes — barbers, garbage collectors, shopkeepers — who became millionaires through careful financial discipline. Their secret? Keeping expenses low. Even Fortune 500 companies are always trying to trim expenses; wise seminary students will as well.

One obstacle for this generation of students is that without realizing it, we have become accustomed to a luxurious life. Designer clothes, the latest smartphone, high speed internet, satellite TV, Netflix subscriptions, laptop computers, and $5 lattes would have been seen as extravagant luxuries in generations past, but today, most students think of such things as essential. Prior generations, frankly, were tougher. They were accustomed to routine self-denial. Air conditioning was only for the hottest months. They grew their own food. Going into debt for a car you couldn't pay cash for was frowned upon.

The point? We all have plenty of room to save if we're just willing to make the hard choices to deny ourselves. Consider these ideas:

- Drive a $2500 car instead of a $25,000 car.
- Get a dumb phone instead of a smart phone. Use a discount carrier.
- Computers are necessities for school these days, but how about a Chromebook instead of a MacBook Pro?
- Turn your AC up a few degrees.
- Sell your TV and cancel your cable. You have too much reading to do anyway.

- Make your coffee at home, except on special occasions.
- Instead of nights out, invite friends in for games and potluck.
- Make your house an internet-free oasis for rest and relationships.
- Coupons, baby.
- Are $9 organic tomatoes at Whole Foods *really* worth it?

Treat it as a game. What can I live without for a few years? Start with the choices that will free up the most money (housing and cars) and add the least amount of stress.

Track Every Single Dollar

One common denominator exists among people who struggle with money. They don't like to talk about their finances and they don't like to budget. By contrast, wealthy people seek out the best advice, and pay the closest attention to how they manage their money.

Small expenses add up to big burdens, so it is important for students to track every dollar they have. One advantage of the digital revolution is that tools for budgeting and tracking money are easier to use and more accessible than ever.

1. Mobile Apps

Apps like Mint, Buxfer, and Personal Finance all allow students to keep a budget and monitor accounts at the swipe of a finger. It is incredibly easy to track all of your expenses. These apps even will automatically link your accounts to track income. During set up, they often give you the opportunity to set goals for saving and budgeting. Do it!

These powerful tools will help you get a handle on your money quite easily.

2. Computer / Online Software

If you prefer a desktop option, there are downloadable software solutions and free cloud based services, too. You might consider Excel as a low-cost option. There are thousands of pre-made budgeting templates that will fit your needs. If none of those suit you, you can make your own.

3. Envelope System

Apps and software may not hold you as accountable as the classic old-school solution: the envelope system. When you get paid, you take that money and distribute preset amounts into envelopes designated for each spending category (food, clothes, entertainment, miscellaneous, etc.). When you run out of money, you can't spend any more.

Common Challenges

Students establishing their first budget often don't know how much to allocate to each category when they start. If you will track your expenses for the first three months and put some time on narrowing down each category to a specific dollar amount, you will have your budget squared away by month three or four.

Another area where students falter in their budgets is the "miscellaneous" category, which can become a dumping ground for hidden expenses. The point of a budget is to have our income and expenses balance perfectly. If you are struggling to make it balance when you start, dig deeper in your miscellaneous expenses.

Every dollar counts, so start tracking!

Emergency Fund

The very first step to financial freedom is establishing an emergency fund: at least $1000 set aside to handle unexpected expenses like a car repair, a medical emergency, or an unexpected trip home for a family funeral. Every student needs one. Without it, your best efforts at controlling expenses and debt can get derailed at the first circumstance.

The goal is to save $1000 as fast as possible, put it somewhere safe and accessible, and then to leave it alone.

If you have an emergency fund already, fantastic! You are ahead of the game, and can start eliminating debt. If not, then trim expenses, save like mad, or even get a side job and focus every dollar on establishing your emergency fund.

You can reach this goal relatively easy. Many people, even on the tightest of budgets can accomplish it in one to three months. The emergency fund (and the process of developing it), will function as the cornerstone upon which you will build healthy financial habits.

Persevere

Once you've learned these principles and taken these first steps, keep making small, right decisions. Be consistent. Establish your emergency fund, knock out debt using the debt eliminator, avoid more debt, and increase your income. Then, continue to live on less than you earn while you save, invest, and give the rest.

17
Give Yourself a Raise

Let's start by thinking ahead. You're fresh out of seminary, married, and working at your local church. Five years from now, your family has grown and you now have four kids. You have gotten a $5,000 raise from the church, but with four kids that raise hasn't helped you as much as you hoped it would. In fact, all things considered, money is tighter than ever. Worse, there is no possibility of a $20,000 or $30,000 raise from the small or mid-size church you are serving. What can you do, except join the throng of pastors jostling to be hired by a larger church in a richer community?

Standard ways of increasing your income are generating added value to your current position so we can ask for a raise, creating passive income to supplement your salary, or getting an additional part-time job. People in ministry often have to get creative to increase their income. Ministry just doesn't pay that well.

One creative solution you could try is to start a "side hustle." A side hustle is a moneymaking business you pursue alongside your regular job. At first glance, you may be intimidated by the cost and risk involved with starting a business, but there's good news: starting and running your own business has never been more affordable or easier than it is today.

You may be wondering what this has to do with surviving seminary. Sure, entrepreneurial types start businesses to make money and pursue their passions. But seminary students are already doing what they are passionate about—serving the Lord. So why would a seminary student start a business? Isn't that a diversion from the real work of ministry?

Here are a few reasons it might make sense.

1. **Most students have passions and skills that range beyond ministry.**

Sure, you can use your graphic design skill to make the church look good, but you could also have private clients and serve businesses in the community. If you're an expert in jiu jitsu, you could offer classes at church, but why not in the community? A talented administrator could help the church organize its systems, but lots of businesses need that, as well, and will pay handsomely for it.

2. **Financial independence keeps you free to follow the Lord's leading.**

Sometimes full-time pastors and church staff members get stuck. They are serving a church that doesn't want to grow and is unresponsive to their leadership, but when that church is paying your family's bills, you may not be able to leave when you want to leave, especially if your only training and experience is in ministry. Being financially independent of a church gives you the freedom to follow the Lord's leading at any moment.

Having a separate income stream will also give you the capacity to take up new or emerging ministry opportunities like planting a church, ministering in an underprivileged community, or making disciples in an unreached country.

3. Many ministry positions don't pay well.

A few talented leaders can earn a handsome salary by leading large churches or developing a book/speaking/consulting practice to support themselves.

The vast majority of pastors, however, have to learn to get by on less, earning what is basically a teacher's salary and often depending on their spouses to bring in the rest their family needs.

4. Bi-vocational ministry provides a wide-open field of ministry.

Bivocational ministry, once looked upon as second-class ministry, is becoming increasingly popular and effective in many contexts. There are hundreds of small churches that cannot afford full-time staff, but would thrive under bivocational leadership. Rich communities can pay their pastors well, but who will serve the poor, the immigrants, the trailer parks, and ghettos? Those people need pastors, too. New church plants, which are desperately needed, are more likely to survive if they do not have to sustain full-time staff at a middle-class lifestyle.

Bivocational ministers, like the Apostle Paul, are increasingly becoming the multiplying engine that drives disciple-making movements around the world.

Bivocational pastors enjoy many benefits. Working a side hustle or a secular job can often provide a stronger income for your family. Better yet, bivocational ministers do not have time for anything except the essentials of ministry: no more endless committee meetings, catering to interest groups, and energy wasters. There just isn't time for anything except laser-focused gospel ministry.

As cultural hostility to Christianity increases in the West, it is entirely possible that religious liberty will erode to the point that churches lose federal tax exemptions. If that happens, thousands of churches will no longer be able to afford full-time ministry staff. Bi-vocational ministry may well be thrust on many pastors and churches as their only means of survival.

It's Not as Hard as You Think

You might be intimidated by the cost and risk involved with starting a business. In days past, starting a business meant you needed manufactured goods, a service, a storefront, a marketing strategy, and a good grasp supply and demand. You could expect to spend well in excess of a hundred thousand dollars just to get started.

But times have changed. As Chris Guillebeau demonstrated in his book *The $100 Startup*, it is possible to start a profitable business for the price of a nice night on the town.

In fact, in today's gig economy, side hustles are becoming commonplace. The number of households reporting income from different sources has skyrocketed in the past decade. There are various side hustles that can be effective, but for ministers, the best choices are those that provide passive income, flexible schedules, and low time demands.

I encourage you to develop an income stream outside of ministry. It could be a product, a service, or a home-based business.

Here's how to get started:

1. Brainstorm and Research Ideas

Start with yourself. Are you an expert in something? What skills do you have? What markets do you know? One interest or skill can generate lots of ideas.

For instance, if you are a beast in the gym, you could do personal training. Or, maybe you could create and sell workout programs for people. Or you could start a blog reviewing sports nutrition products and earn money through affiliate links. You could host pop up weekend workouts at public parks.

If you're bilingual, you could offer translation services for local businesses, proofread translated copy for real estate agencies, provide voiceovers for commercials, or tutor immigrants trying to learn English.

If you're a flea market master, you could find cheap novelty items on the weekend and sell them online at a profit. If you know how to market, there is an ocean of products you can sell and dropship to customers without ever having to maintain inventory.

Can you develop a product like woodcrafts or custom sewn potholders? Could you develop an online course such as simple shortcuts to selling your house at a good price? Can you provide consulting services? You can consult on almost anything you know a lot about.

Develop a list of side hustle ideas (try for a dozen), then look around and see if anyone else is making money doing something on your list. How much are they charging? How are they advertising? You might take what they are doing successfully and do it in another area or for a different demographic.

Your best idea will be one that is easy to set up, profitable, and most appealing to potential customers.

2. Run the numbers

First, create a half page business proposal. First, the basics: What will you sell? Who will buy it? How will it benefit them?

Second, think through the numbers: How much will it cost you to get started? What do you need (e.g. business cards, website, an 800 number, any specialized equipment?)? What will you charge? How will you get paid?

Third, consider how you will market your side hustle: How will you get the word out? Who are your customers? Where will you find them? How will you reach them?

3. Get Started

If you're nervous about your idea, you're in good company. Everyone who starts something gets the jitters. The best strategy is to start before you're ready and learn as you go. Not sure how to take photos for high school seniors? Advertise yourself for cheap on Craigslist, get a couple of clients, and learn as you go. Not sure if anyone is interested in your window washing business? Knock on doors or visit businesses until you get your first yes. If you ask 100 and no one seems interested, change your approach or abandon your idea.

If you're working through an online platform, test ads on Facebook or Google and see if anyone clicks through. If no one does, change your strategy.

When you get your first customer, throw yourself a party, and then go get another one.

4. Incorporate

Once your business gets going, make it official. This is a side hustle, but you are starting a company. Set it up properly the first time so you don't run into unforeseen obstacles down the road.

In Florida, for example, entrepreneurs can login into sunbiz.org and create an LLC in less than 10 minutes. If you're not sure which incorporation model is best, do some research or get professional advice.

5. Play Long Ball

It's a side hustle, so don't expect to make $50,000 your first year. Your first couple of years are where you learn. Take notes from mentors and pay close attention to what's working (what's not!). Track your progress intently, and be ready to make adjustments big and small.

Create, Launch, Evaluate, and Adjust.

When Should You Start?

The best time to start your side hustle is before you enroll in seminary. If you can develop an income stream before you hit the books, it will relieve some of the financial pressure of seminary.

You can start a business during seminary, but beware of the time factor. The time drain of starting a new venture on top of everything else could prove overwhelming. If you have a promising business idea, you might consider scaling back to part time for a while or taking a semester off to give you the time you need to get it up and running.

Even if you wait until after graduation, it is still a good idea to start a side hustle while you're in ministry. It can supplement your income and help you pay off student loans.

Extras:

Go to seminarysurvivalguide.com/book-extras for extra resources, including book recommendations for starting side businesses.

BEWARE OF TIME WASTERS

18

Seminary Time Waster #1: Procrastination

We've all been there: some assignment is looming that we really don't want to do, so instead, we'll do anything else. We'll read a book other than the one we need to, or call a friend, or start playing a video game, or take a nap. I've even done housework as a way of procrastinating! Putting off things that we dread is a very human temptation, but is completely self-destructive.

Here are a few practical tips on overcoming procrastination. Some of these tips will work well for you, others won't. Pick and choose as you will.

Don't think so much. Act!

In his helpful article, "Do It Now!", Steve Pavlina cites W. Clement Stone, a giant in the insurance industry, who would lead his employees to chant together "Do it now, Do it now!" at the beginning of each day. When you're tempted to put off a task because you don't like it or it's going to be hard, stop yourself, and say loudly three times, "Do it now! Do it now! Do it now!" (Really! It works.)

> "There is a tremendous cost in putting things off because you will mentally revisit them again and again, which can add up to an enormous amount of wasted time. Thinking and planning are important, but action is far more important. You don't get paid for your thoughts and plans — you only get paid for your results. When in doubt, act boldly, as if it were impossible to fail. In essence, it is."
>
> – S. Pavlina

Give preference to action over thought. Start! If you don't know how to clean up the room, just start cleaning. If you don't know what to eat for dinner, just start grabbing whatever's in the fridge and start eating. If you don't know what to write the paper on, just start writing. Get yourself into a creative zone, and the ideas will emerge.

Break big projects down into smaller chunks

Sometimes imposing tasks like a big paper can overwhelm you if you don't know where to start. Paralysis becomes procrastination, while the deadlines creep ever nearer.

Instead, face it head on. Sit down and break that big project into bite-size pieces. For instance, if you have to write a paper, break it down into manageable steps, and estimate the time each will take.

- Look at the list of topics, and choose one. (10 minutes)
- Go to the library and find your preliminary list of sources (2 hours)
- Being doing your primary source reading (4 hours)
- Brainstorm a thesis (30 minutes)
- Write a first draft (2-4 hours)
- Edit, do supporting research (2 hours)
- Polish final draft (2-3 hours)

Then each of the tasks on your list can be placed into your daily calendar over the next few weeks.

See? That wasn't so bad after all. You'd be surprised at how much freedom that comes from just a little bit of strategic thinking.

Single Handling

Another procrastination elimination strategy is single handling. That is, touch each task only once and finish it the first time. When you get your mail, handle everything in it immediately. Pitch junk mail, pay bills, and deal with personal correspondence right away. Don't just drop in on the table where you'll have to come back and give it more of your time.

Email works the same way. Don't leave things festering in your inbox. When you sit down to handle your email, handle it. Reply, make decisions, forward messages, make calendar appointments. Make the first time you read an email the last time you read it. (Google "Inbox zero" to find more tips and advice.)

The 60-second rule

Do you procrastinate on making decisions? Give yourself a 60-second rule for making all decisions. That is, once you have all the facts you need, why should it take you any longer than that? Analysis becomes paralysis quickly.

If you're hesitant, try this: make the decision, one way or another, and then don't do anything about it, just sit on it for an hour or two or a day or two, and see how it feels. Then you can put it into action. It's much better than indecision and endless pondering back and forth, which will only waste time.

Make the cut

Too often, we let time slip away because we are for whatever reason unwilling to make a decision or start moving. The word "decision" is related to "incision". When you decide, you make a cut: you cut something in, you cut something out. Stop worrying over what cut away when you decide. Make the cut! And do it now!

Eat the Frog

Mark Twain is famous for saying that if you have to eat a frog, the best time to do it is first thing in the morning. "Eating the frog" means doing the task you're dreading. When you think about all you have to do, that one thing you're avoiding is the frog. If you don't eat the frog, the frog will eat you—meaning that the task gets bigger and more intimidating the longer you avoid it.

Do your most dreaded task before you do anything else. Eat that frog and get it out of the way. In truth, the hardest thing about any work we dread is just getting started.

Do it now!

Extras:

Go to seminarysurvivalguide.com/book-extras for extra resources, including Steve Pavlina's original article, "Do It Now!"

19

Seminary Time Waster #2: The Digital Black Hole

Our computers and cell phones are gateways to endless distraction, which is a low value use of our time.

First it was email. Then came websites and blogs. Then Facebook, Twitter, Instagram, Snapchat, WhatsApp, and others began to vie for our valuable time. Clickbait beckons endlessly. Plus, there's shopping, video games, pornography, and endless fascinating articles on every subject. It's easy to fall down the digital black hole and waste hours and hours of time. All these digital channels will make you their slave if you aren't careful.

Here are some suggestions, culled from multiple sources, about reducing technological time drain.

Avoid all digital engagement in the early morning. Don't leave your phone next to your bed at night. If you roll out of bed and check email or social media first thing, it will suck your brain into a hole.

Check your email and social media only at designated times each day. Tim Ferriss, a master thinker in this area, suggests as a starting point to check email no more than twice a day (11am and 4pm), and never first thing in the morning. If check your email first when you get to work or to the library to study, it will suck your energy and concentration away in nothing flat. Resist the temptation. Choose ahead of time when you'll check it, and stick to it.

Set Time Limits. When checking email, reading blogs or browsing Instagram, give yourself a time limit. Like watching television, hours can go by before you know it, while vital projects are patiently awaiting your attention.

Use a timer. When you sit down to clear your email and catch up on social media, set a timer for 10 or 15 minutes. When it goes off, climb out of the digital hole and get going on something productive. It may seem silly, but that little discipline has saved me lots of time.

Unsubscribe from email lists. Every purchase you make online rewards you with daily email from that vendor, for the rest of your life. Every month or so, go through and unsubscribe. It will reduce the digital noise in your inbox. You may not realize how calming it will be.

Quit the news. I love the news, but none of it is really new. It's the same news as yesterday, only the names and dates have changed. Try quitting the news altogether. I bet you won't miss it. If something really important happens, someone will tell you about it.

Stop trying to keep up with everything. Even in the world of church and theology, there are way more articles, trends, and developments out there than you could ever keep up with. Don't try. It's more important that you really focus on your studies, your time with God, and your family and friends.

Go on regular social media fasts. Take one or two days a week, say Saturday and Sunday, and just stay off social media. Use those days to invest in real relationships with real people. An occasional week off wouldn't hurt, either. When you take vacations, wait till you return to post pictures and update people on your adventures. Please don't find yourself at the Grand Canyon staring at your phone watching cat videos and reading political blogs. There are smartphone apps (like Self Control, Freedom, FocusWriter, etc.) that can help. Use them.

When you're in seminary, time is a scarce resource. Guard it ferociously.

20

Be Unavailable, Like Jesus.

Completing a seminary education requires deliberate and sustained thinking — the kind that is impossible in high-interruption environments. You should aim for long, uninterrupted blocks of study time. I'd recommend a minimum of 90 minutes. You should have enough time to get "into the zone" of the reading or assignment you're working on. Your productivity goes way up when you're in those intense, creative mental flows.

By contrast, in high-interruption environments, you can't get anything done, because you can't get gain any momentum. It's like a runner being stopped every 100 yards to have a conversation. In corporate America, a staggering 25% of all work time is spent handling interruptions and switching from one task to another. After 40% of these interruptions, people never return to what they were doing before the interruption.

The worst interrupter of all time is the cell phone.

Unless you manage it wisely, your cell phone allows anyone in the world to interrupt you at any time. Availability is one thing, slavery is another.

Set times when you will be unavailable. When you are studying, praying, or with your family, your cell phone should not be able to distract you. Turn it off or put it in sleep mode.

I once found that every time I tried to watch a movie, my phone would blow up. I used to feel obligated to answer and could never get through a movie. Ridiculous. One strategy I like: leave the cell phone on silent in another room. I can't hear it ring, but when I pause the movie for snacks or a bathroom break, I can check for missed calls or messages (if I want) and return them (if I want).

Spouses and availability

Communicate with your spouse about your need to avoid interruptions when studying. If you prioritize her needs in the ways that you should, then she'll most likely protect you as much as she can. She can call if it's really urgent.

On a date? Leave your phone in the car, and give your date your full attention. If you have kids with a sitter, they'll call your wife's phone if they need to anyway.

Use your free secretary

I love this idea: think of your phone like it's your virtual assistant. Didn't know that a FREE secretary came with that cell phone, did you? It's all a matter of perspective. Let your cell phone "receptionist" gather messages (email, voicemail, and text) and check them when it makes sense to do so. Return only messages that really need it. Try to train people who communicate with you to leave the information you need in the message. "Hey, call me back" is not an acceptable message. Let them know.

When you get the awful conversation starter text "Hey, what's up," ignore it. You'll get sucked in. Reply hours later, "Sorry, I was busy."

Try a voicemail greeting like this: "This is Mark. I'm not available now. If you have information for me, feel free to text me at this number, or send an email to mark@gmail.com. If you'd like a call back, please leave your name, number, and the purpose of your call. I generally return calls in the early afternoon. Due to family time, I do not return messages on Saturdays. Thanks for calling."

Email autoresponders can work the same way. "Thanks for your email. I generally reply to emails at 11am and 4pm, Monday through Thursday. If you need more immediate assistance, call the church office at 555-5555." Something along those lines will save you tremendous time.

You get the idea. You need boundaries, so set them and enforce them. Other people will not respect your boundaries unless you do. They also will not respect your boundaries if they do not know where they are. Communicate those boundaries clearly.

When you leave messages for others, give them a specific time to call you back. This avoids phone tag. "This is Mark, returning your call. My number is 555-5555. The best time to reach me is between 3 and 5."

Other quick ideas that may help:

- Turn off all notifications for email and social media: no icon, no ding, nothing. Check when you want, period.
- Silence notifications for group texts (What a relief!).
- When I really need to be uninterrupted, I go where people can't find me. I get drop-in interruptions way too much at my office.
- At seminary, beware of the "social corners" of the library. You know, where the gabby extroverts like to hang out and not work. Don't go there. Socialize when it's time to socialize; work when it's time to work.

Be Unavailable, Like Jesus.

Other people will not understand or respect your very great need for sustained theological reflection or uninterrupted time in prayer. Learn to set those boundaries now, and learn to make others adjust to them.

Jesus did not ask permission to go away by himself and pray. He just did it. When people needed him, they just had to deal with it until he got back.

I think that's a pretty good example.

21

Fix All Your Time Problems with One Decision

Let's begin with a dry statistic. The average American watches 5 hours, 4 minutes of television every day.[ix] Five hours seems benign until you start doing some math. Five hours a day translates to 1,849 hours per year. That's *eleven weeks a year* of television. Eleven weeks!!

If you have the courage, you can solve all of your time problems with one hard decision. Get rid of your TV. I'm serious. Sell, it, trash it, give it away. Cancel your cable, and turn off your Netflix account. The upside: you gain the time equivalent of over five years' worth of vacation handed to you on a silver platter. Eleven free weeks *every year*! Ditch the TV and you might never have a time problem again.

If you (or your spouse) isn't quite ready for that step, I understand. TV is fine for a little entertainment or downtime, but it is a time waster of which you should remain very aware.

Here are my recommendations for managing TV-time:

Pick one or two shows, and stick to them. Leave the TV off the rest of the time. Pick those your family enjoys together, and when they're over, turn it off.

Better yet, DVR your shows and watch w/o commercials. A one-hour drama can be seen in 41 minutes this way. If you watch one season of a typical show, you'll have spent **eight hours watching commercials**. Wouldn't you rather be doing something else?

Don't watch TV news or morning shows. They are slanted, trite, and horribly inaccurate. Pick a favorite news website, scan the headlines once a day (or better, once a week), and you can be done in 3 minutes instead of 30. Or get the Sunday paper (old school) and spend Sunday afternoons lazily in bed with your wife. That's good multitasking right there.

But the best recommendation: don't watch TV at all. Completely eliminate it.

Listen to John Piper:

> Turn off the television. It is not necessary for relevance. And it is a deadly place to rest the mind. Its pervasive banality, sexual innuendo, and God-ignoring values have no ennobling effects on the preacher's soul. It kills the spirit. It drives God away. It quenches prayer. It blanks out the Bible. It cheapens the soul. It destroys spiritual power. It defiles almost everything. I have taught and

preached for twenty years now and never owned a television. It is unnecessary for most of you, and it is spiritually deadly for all of you.[x]

Early in my ministry, I decided to put the TV away for the summer, just as an experiment. I unplugged it and crammed it into a closet. After about two weeks of withdrawal, I decided I loved it. Instead of TV, I read more and exercised more, and became smarter and fitter. It was a great decision.

Try going without TV as an experiment. Start with a month — long enough to go through withdrawal and settle in to a new pattern. Take your TV to your mom's house, put it in a closet, and see how it goes. You might find it's the best thing you ever did.

STRENGTHEN RELATIONSHIPS

22

The Hidden Spiritual Danger of Seminary

I entered seminary with many of the common illusions most students have. I thought it would be a spiritually vibrant and intense place, full of people who were overflowing with passion for Christ.

One day in a study group with guys from my Hebrew class, we got in a conversation about scriptural interpretation. A prominent church leader had shared in chapel how he had made a major life decision based on a particular verse of Scripture…and by the rules we were studying at the time, we agreed that he'd interpreted the Scripture incorrectly.

Somewhere in that conversation one of the guys made a remark I'll never forget. He said, "Interpreting the Bible properly takes so much difficult study that I don't even bother to read my Bible devotionally anymore."

I agreed with him that proper interpretation has its challenges, but disagreed that the Bible is therefore inscrutable. I asked him, "You mean to tell me that Farmer Jones can't sit down with his Bible and his morning coffee, pray that God will speak to him through it and expect reliably to hear from God?"

He said, "No, that's not possible."

Wow. I chalked it up to him being one of those weird guys that you're bound to run into anywhere. After a while, the others left the room, and I stayed talking to another friend, a normal, conservative guy, the kind of guy you'd want to be on a church staff with you.

I was complaining about the weird guy, and to my surprise, he said, "Well, to be honest with you, I don't read my Bible devotionally any more either."

He paused.

"And neither does John, or Keith, or...." He went on to name about six guys from his floor that he knew for a fact had abandoned daily time in prayer and Bible Study.

I was amazed. We talked more. He had been very faithful in personal devotion in college, but somehow just stopped.

My friends, who were immersed in the in-depth study of the word of God, had completely abandoned a devotional pursuit of God. They started studying God and stopped loving Him.

I went on to discover that this happens quite frequently among seminary students. Honestly, I struggled very much with my devotional life during seminary. By God's mercy, I managed to keep my habits of prayer maintained, but seminary was a dry and difficult time.

Knowledge Is Not Life

One of the dangers of seminary is that so much emphasis and time is spent on the expansion of your knowledge base, that students neglect their devotion to and obedience to God. The simple southerners in my home church in Florida cautioned me: "Don't let seminary ruin you." I knew what they meant. Stories abounded of young men who went to seminary fired up to change the world for Jesus, and returned cold and lifeless, all their zeal dissolved in the acid of theological debates and parsing of verbs. They got immense knowledge and lost spiritual vibrancy.

In an academic environment, it's easy to make the assumption that knowledge is what qualifies you for ministry. It's not. What qualifies you for ministry is the life and calling of God in you. It is the power of the Holy Spirit who has brought you from death to life.

Remember, "This 'knowledge' puffs up, but love builds up. If anyone imagines that he knows something, he does not yet know as he ought to know. But if anyone loves God, he is known by God." (1 Corinthians 8:1-3, NIV)

That's not to say that knowledge is bad. It's not. There are things you need to know, and seminary is for learning. I didn't even know how to think until I went to seminary.

But be warned, knowledge is not life. In fact, when knowledge is pursued in place of spiritual growth, it leads to spiritual *decline*.

Knowledge alone makes you a Pharisee. The gift of spiritual life makes you a Christian. Jesus did not come to make us smart. He came to make us live.

The way I think of it now is that knowledge fuels our love for God and others, which then propels our obedience to God's commands. Obedience then produces a kind of experiential knowledge, which further fuels our love and propels us to greater obedience.

So as you're studying diligently in seminary, let your increasing knowledge fuel an increasing love of God and his people. Leading God's people is not about being smart. Christian leaders are shepherds, not professors. Knowledge is useful, even necessary. But it is not life.

Here are some suggestions:

Maintain A Devotional Time with God. No matter what time pressures come to bear, make this a non-negotiable of your day. Time with God should be like showering or brushing your teeth: no matter how busy we are, we never skip our physical maintenance and grooming. Make it the same with your walk with God. No matter what, always take a few minutes to give God your undivided attention.

Don't be a Spiritual Olympian. Time with God every day doesn't have to be super long or super profound. If you're reading devotionally and praying daily for 10 minutes, that's better than nothing at all. In an ideal world, you'd have the liberty to spend more like 30-60 minutes with God every day, but we don't live in an ideal world. Don't think that simple and brief moments with God are inferior.

Pray over assignments. We usually think of time with God as separate from everything else we do, and Jesus' example shows us by example that time alone with God is important. However, Jesus carried his connection with God into every moment of ministry. Take time to pray before reading and writing sessions. Invite the Lord's presence into everything you're doing.

Find a spiritual mentor. Mentors are notoriously hard to find, especially if the idea is for regularly scheduled intentional time. Anyone with a walk with God you respect, however, can be a mentor of sorts, even if you only have one conversation or meet for coffee when you can squeeze it in. Conversation about the Lord and your soul with people outside of the seminary context can be especially helpful.

Make times for personal spiritual retreats. In between semesters is ideal to take a day or two to hike into the woods, or find a secret place to renew your intimacy with God apart from textbooks and exams. I took a semester off halfway through my M.Div. because I was worn out. Relieving the pressure of school for a while can help restore your soul.

A mentor of mine said that if you have the love of God and the respect of your spouse, not much else matters, including seminary and ministry.

23
Relationships Are More Important Than You Think

The most important benefit of seminary might be the people you meet, not the things you learn.

Imagine yourself in a new student orientation meeting with dozens or hundreds of other fellow students. Sitting around you are the people who will be leading God's church in your generation. A few are clowns. Others will wash out and not continue in ministry. But some of your fellow students will become highly influential leaders in the church and the Kingdom all over the world.

Some will become pastors of large and influential churches. Some will become professors or even presidents of seminaries. Some will pioneer new missions and movements in places all around the world.

Imagine yourself sitting in the first week of classes one semester. Your professors, who are paid to teach you and give you some of their attention, might be among the top ten scholars in the world in their particular fields of study.

You really need to get to know these people, for two reasons. First of all, they are just amazing and fascinating. People at seminary have to pass two important qualifications to even be there: they have to love God and they have to be academically competent. This means, on the whole, that your fellow students will be both spiritually and intellectually strong. Who wouldn't want friends like that?

Second, never underestimate the importance of networking. The saying is true: "It's not what you now, it's who you know." Most ministry positions are filled through relational networks. A strong network of personal connection increases both your own prospects in ministry and the value you will bring to any church or organization you serve.

Suggestions:

Meet 100 people. During your first semester, introduce yourself around a lot. Make it a priority. See someone you don't know, smile, extend your hand, and introduce yourself. You will not become fast friends will all of them, but with a few, you might. Meet fellow students, who, in a few short years will disperse to places of influence all over the world. Meet professors, remembering that it is their job to give you some of their attention. Don't neglect the networking opportunities in your local church, either. Knowing ordinary, non-seminary people can be a resource for your sanity and your family. It can even help connect you to reliable people when you have a non-seminary related need, for example, insurance or car repairs.

Take initiative. Someone has to be the first to talk; it might as well be you. If you take the passive route, and wait for friends to drift your way, you might find yourself lonely. Be the leader and take the first step. Introduce yourself. Offer to buy coffee. Drop in on your professors early in the semester during office hours, and ask one or two good questions — they will remember.

Add value. As you meet people, discover ways you can serve or help them. Two of the biggest things you can offer are resources and relationships. What have you seen or read that could help them? Who do you know that they need to know?

Leverage social media. As you meet people, connect with them on social media. This gives both of you mutual access to each other. You can stay aware of what's happening with them, and they with you. Pay attention, and look for strategic ways and times to be helpful.

Express care. In the days before social media, I noticed that an acquaintance of mine in a philosophy class did not show up for our midterm exam. I got his number from another student and called to see if he was ok. Turns out he had been in an auto accident and simultaneously discovered he was diabetic. He was blown away at my small expression of care. That moment of care blossomed into a friendship where we spent many hours together talking philosophy and religion. We took a trip to Ireland together, and I was in his wedding. Even small expressions of care are rare enough that they stand out.

Be generous. One of my professors had to drive to another city for a meeting after our class, but was exhausted from travel and illness. I volunteered to drive him up and back so he could snooze in the car. He gratefully accepted my offer, and I got several hours of uninterrupted time with him. He later served on my dissertation committee.

Connect even if you're an online student. It takes a bit more effort, but even distance or online students can connect with people. Use the bulletin board or chat features of your school's learning software. Send an introductory email to fellow students, and offer to swap notes, or host a group video chat to help everyone connect.

Forming new friendships isn't on the curriculum for seminary, but it ought to be. Don't miss the opportunity to form relationships; it's more important than you think.

Extras:

Go to seminarysurvivalguide.com/book-extras for extra resources and book recommendations.

24
Single at Seminary

At seminary, singleness is a great advantage. Single people have freedom and bandwidth for school and ministry that married students do not have. Frankly, seminary is easier for single people. You have more time to devote to study and ministry. Married students, especially those with kids, have it much harder than you.

Single people, however, often feel the pressure from evangelical church culture to get married. Churches still prefer married candidates for ministry positions. When is the last time you heard of a large church or big ministry led by a single person? I don't remember either.

So let's address a few issues for single people.

Redeem the season

Singleness is often taken as an opportunity for self-indulgence. Some single friends I've had have used all their time on themselves: sleeping in, movies, concerts, Netflix, whatever. There was no sense that their available time and energy ought to be spent on serving others, making themselves available for ministry, or for studying beyond the basics of what was required of them.

If you're single, you have more relational space than your married friends do. Use it, first, to minister to others. You can have conversations with college students who need to talk late at night when married people need to be home in bed. You can join a community running group and befriend people far from God.

Second, single students should use some of their time to find and develop rich, deep godly friendships with people who love God and have dedicated their lives to serving and pleasing Him. Most pastors report that close friendships are hard to come by in ministry, so having a stable of good friends early on can serve you the rest of your days.

Also, since being at seminary is such a privilege, consider that singleness gives you an opportunity to go further than most in one area of study. You could dig deep in Greek or Hebrew or Systematic Theology by reading and studying beyond the requirements of class. Leveraging your singleness in this way could help you develop an uncommon aptitude in these subjects, which would benefit your ministry for the rest of your life.

Looking for Romance?

If you are single and satisfied to remain single for the foreseeable future, then follow the pattern of Paul, and pour yourself into ministry.

If you want to get married, however, you should do the same thing: pour yourself into ministry. Then, as you do so, look to either side of you and see who catches your eye. Men in ministry will want the kind of wives who see ministry as part of their calling, as well. The best place to find that person is on the front lines of ministry.

So take mission trips with seminary or college groups. Find a ministry team in your area that is serving among refugees, the homeless, or addicts. Find a coed group doing ministry together, plug in, and look around.

I know many couples who met through online dating sites and apps. There are both advantages and dangers in online dating, so tread carefully and wisely. If you go this route, try to move the relationship from the digital world to the real world as quickly as possible.

You should definitely be accountable for all aspects of your dating life to a godly friend or mentor, preferably someone with more age and experience than you. A major relational mistake can injure your long-term opportunities in ministry.

Pray diligently for God to lead you to a godly spouse. I encourage you to pray this way not just by yourself, but together with select friends and mentors.

You may be feeling the pressure of the ticking graduation clock and really want to get married before you graduate. If it's important enough to you, you might consider shifting down to part-time or taking a semester off if you have a relationship developing toward engagement.

Finally, beware of "choice paralysis." The digital age gives us so many choices, that it's hard to be certain we're making the best choice. This mentality leaks over into relationships, too. If you are dating someone who is a potential spouse, but find yourself hesitating to get married because you're uncertain if they are the "right one" or if another one will come along that might be a better match, you might be suffering from choice paralysis.

Disney is not real life. There are no perfect mates, because there are no perfect people. Pray, seek counsel, find a match, and get married.

But until then, take full advantage of your singleness. Even if it is only a short season for you, make the most of it. And if God grants you contentment to be single for a long season or even a lifetime, use it for His glory.

25
Protecting Your Marriage at Seminary

More marriages fail in seminary and ministry than you might think. The pressure cooker of seminary is only a prelude to the stresses of life in ministry. Pastors have one of the highest stress occupations, and often feel lonely and isolated. The stress will affect your marriage.[xi]

Here are some suggestions:

Your relationship with your spouse must be a higher priority than anything except your relationship with God. Priority means that you will have to say no to other things to protect your time with her. This includes your coursework at seminary. Getting a B with a good marriage is far better than an A with a frustrated wife.

Schedule your time together, and protect that time like it's a final exam. A weekly date night (or even monthly if you work two jobs) is a genius idea. Give your spouse your undivided attention during these times: TV off, cell phone in the car.

Sex night. It may sound ultra-nerdy to plan time for physical intimacy, but spontaneity can be hard to find amid the stresses and time pressures of classes and multiple jobs, compounded with sheer exhaustion.

Spend a little money. Seminarians are usually poor, but splurging strategically on your wife for small pleasures (Dairy Queen or a small gift) is a good idea.

Make sure you agree about the importance of seminary. If your spouse supports your work toward the degree, sees the value in it, and sees herself as a partner with you in achieving it, it will be a huge advantage. Discuss it often, dream together, and pray together about it. These discussions ideally should begin before you apply to start, and should persist all the way through.

Try to do seminary work when it does not compete with family time: between classes, early in the morning before others get up, or late, after they go to bed.

Your wife may not share your enthusiasm about everything you are learning. Do not monopolize your time together by discussing the arcana of Greek exegesis or theological debates. Include her, but make sure she is not your only seminary discussion partner. You'll wear her out.

If you get married during seminary, take time off to work on your new marriage: a summer, a semester, or even a year. There is biblical precedent for this practice (See Deuteronomy 24:5).

Remember that you're not the only one growing. Your wife is, too, in her job, her parenting, her spiritual growth. You should be as enthusiastic to encourage and support her in those things as you'd like her to support your pursuit of a degree.

Make friends with couples who aren't in seminary. Your local church is great for place to start. If you are a young couple, find an older couple to be friends with that can adopt you and offer wisdom and support.

Plan to be together at strategic moments. Seminary can breed a life apart, full of "Sorry, I have things to do." Date night is a start, but consider setting a time to pray together every night. It might be important for your marriage to go to bed at the same time every night. If you're able to, sit together in church. And drop everything for birthdays and anniversaries.

If the stress of seminary begins to weigh heavily on your marriage, seminary has to give. Drop a class, take a semester off, or even quit your program entirely to protect your marriage. It may disrupt you or your seminary's neat, four-year curriculum plan, but who cares?

Plan a special celebratory weekend after graduation. After the degree is on the wall, take off and enjoy some well-deserved, uninterrupted time together.

✚

AVOID PITFALLS

26
Stumbling at Seminary: Cheating

In an interview with the dean of students at a leading evangelical seminary, I asked about the most common reasons people did not complete seminary. One of his answers was a shock to me: students get caught cheating.

Seminary students have ample opportunity to cheat. You can plagiarize—representing the academic work of others as your own. You can rip off fellow students, sometimes with their cooperation. You can rip off published scholars through failure to provide necessary citations in your written work. You can use forbidden resources on exams. Conjugations written on the palm of your hand? Ever have a take-home, closed-book exam? Only at seminary!

You can dishonestly answer those dreaded blanket questions on your final exam, like:

- Did you read all of your required readings?
- Did you complete assignment X?

Seminaries tend to be more trusting with academic honor codes than their secular counterparts. But students still cheat. No one knows how much cheating goes on, but if we did, I suspect we would be embarrassed.

The spiritual roots of cheating

My systematic theology professor taught us that all sins boil down to either pride or sloth. Cheating is no different. Let's think deeply about this: why would you cheat?

Pride

- You're afraid you cannot pass seminary on your own, and would be ashamed to be found out as academically incapable.
- You believe that the grade you make in class is an evaluation of you, not just your performance, and feel the need to inflate it.
- Making a poor grade is unthinkable, so since you're busy, you take a few shortcuts.
- Since you're capable of making an "A" anyway, why should you be forced to work to prove it?
- Who will know? It doesn't matter anyway.

The common factor in these is pride. The antidote to pride is humility.

- Humility is always chosen. It is never accidental.
- Humility is a choice only you can make. God won't make you humble. His word clearly teaches that we

are to humble ourselves. "Humble yourselves before the Lord, and he will exalt you." (James 4:10, ESV)
- "God opposes the proud." If you've rationalized your cheating out of pride, consider this: Almighty God stands in eternal opposition to your inflated thoughts of yourself.
- "…but gives grace to the humble." There is an unending cascade of grace for those who choose humility. Trust in that future grace.
- If you make a "D" in Biblical Backgrounds, that doesn't mean you're not called of God.
- If you fail a test, it doesn't mean you are a failure.
- If your professor thinks poorly of you, that doesn't mean that God does.

Humility, as I understand it, means taking God's view of us as the true and correct view. This encompasses both the horror of our capacity for sin, and the splendor of the gifts and nobility God has put within us.

We need to have the courage to face the truth about ourselves. We can only do that by being secure in the love and favor of God in Christ. If I know I am deeply loved and approved by God in Christ, then I can handle making a "C".

Sloth

The other major root of cheating is laziness — raw unwillingness to exert effort. You don't want to do the work, so cheating is a shortcut. You cheat not to protect your image of reputation, but simply because you did not want to do the work.

Much like pride, sloth is characterized by rationalizations. We are never so creative as when we're trying to come up with reasons to avoid work. A lazy person will say or believe anything to justify avoidance of exertion.

The effort we're willing to expend in service to God reflects our view of His greatness. If Almighty God in all his glory, power and love can't motivate you to a bit of work and self-denial, then something is seriously wrong. You may need to check your conversion.

If you've cheated:

Repent. In the most literal sense, you need to change your mind about it. Your dishonesty is an offense against the God of truth. Be done with your rationalizations, and acknowledge your sin.

Come Clean. Do this first with a pastor or trusted spiritual advisor; the more mature, the better. Confession is never fun but is cleansing to the soul. Second, come clean with your professor, even if the class is already over. Go to him or her, tell exactly what you did, and submit to whatever instructions you're given.

Find the root. What motivated you to cheat in the first place? Find out. Don't assume that the first answer you come up with off the top of your head is correct, either. This kind of issue is best talked through with a counselor or perceptive spiritual director. Most seminaries have free counseling for students. Go sign up.

Walk in the light. Don't do it anymore. Study hard, do your best, and accept whatever grade you get with grace. Write your own papers. Cite all borrowed material, even if you have to lug back to the library to get the page number. Enjoy the sweet fruit of a clean conscience.

Final warning

If you're willing to cheat in seminary, you'll cheat when you're ministering in a church. You'll eventually be found out, and it will damage the church and the cause of Christ. When it makes the papers, you will drive lost people away from the gospel. The choices you make in the privacy of your head have repercussions that you cannot fathom. Resolve now to live with integrity, no matter what it costs you.

27

Stumbling at Seminary: Laziness

In the face of all the demands of seminary, the temptation to laziness can be acute. I've spoken with a number of students who succumb to laziness, to their own chagrin. They have much to get done, but cannot get themselves to do it.

Often laziness will show up as procrastination. Laziness manifests itself when we choose a distracting or escapist activity instead of the work at hand. For example, many students will choose to spend time on social media, PlayStation, TV, movies, unnecessary reading, or lying inactive on the couch rather than completing an assignment, starting on a paper, or studying for an exam.

Some factors that contribute to laziness:

- Physical exhaustion. Often people with high demand jobs or hours get to the point where they are so physically tired they cannot muster the energy to do something else.
- Lack of endurance. When you begin seminary it usually involves greater time demands than you've faced before. Adjusting to the amount of work to be done can be difficult when you're not accustomed to it.
- Mental Paralysis. I am one who can get mentally paralyzed in the face of too many demands. I'll get overwhelmed and don't know where to begin, so I'll do nothing.
- Depression. Indolence and chronic un-motivation can be a symptom of depression.

Most of the time, however, laziness is just a sinful choice that becomes a pattern in life, regardless of your life circumstances. It is a decision of will. The sin of sloth is about taking more joy in ease than in doing the will or work of God. It is a refusal to execute the responsibilities reasonably expected of us.

Factors we've mentioned above can worsen the temptation, in the same way a married man's temptation to lust is more problematic when his wife is out of town or he's traveling. But the circumstance is not the problem. Our hearts are.

A few theological reminders:

We were created to work. "The Lord God took the man and put him in the garden of Eden to work it and keep it." (Genesis 2:15, ESV)

We are commanded to work. It's easy to forget the Sabbath commandment (which we routinely break) begins with a command to work for six days.

"Six days you shall labor, and do all your work, but the seventh day is a Sabbath to the Lord your God. On it you shall not do any work…" (Exodus 20:9-10a, ESV)

We do need rest. Laziness, however, is not about rest. It's about avoiding exertion.

We were saved to do good works. "For we are his workmanship, created in Christ Jesus for good works, which God prepared beforehand, that we should walk in them." (Ephesians 2:10, ESV)

Remember also the Bible is clear about the results of laziness:

- Fruitlessness (Proverbs 20:4)
- Poor reputation (Proverbs 10:26)
- Lying (Proverbs 22:13)
- Poverty (Proverbs 24:30-34)
- Procrastination (Proverbs 6:9)
- Hindrances (Proverbs 15:19)
- Conceit (Proverbs 26:16)
- Dissatisfaction (Proverbs 13:4)
- Death (Proverbs 21:25)

If you are succumbing to laziness, here are a few suggestions:

Take responsibility. No one is making you lazy; that decision is entirely your own. Don't blame it on anyone or anything but yourself.

Be done with excuses. Your life is not that exceptional. Everyone has a lot to do. Quit whining.

Take initiative. You will only overcome laziness through the exertion of effort on your part.

Look at the big picture of your life. What is it that you want to do? What's your purpose in being at seminary?

Try keeping an activity log for a few days. What exactly ARE you doing? Write down everything you do and how long it takes you. Just being aware of what you actually do during a day can help.

Break things down. If you find yourself overwhelmed, break down your work into hour long chunks, and assign them to your calendar. Then you can focus on just one thing at a time.

Simplify your schedule. If you have too much to do, look for things you can eliminate or delegate.

Get counseling. Laziness can be a symptom of depression. Are you depressed? People in ministry are not immune! Most seminaries have free counseling. Make an appointment.

Go to sleep. If you're tired, sleep. Most Americans, in fact, are acutely sleep deprived. Beware of staying up late watching TV or vegging on the couch. It is not helping you. Go to bed.

Exercise. Done right, exercise is energizing, not tiring. I'm not asking you to run marathons, but a brisk walk will help improve your metabolism and it will get you moving.

Watch your diet. Eating fresh and healthy choices will help feel more energized. Fast food can make you lethargic.

Be with people. It's much easier to be lazy when other people aren't around. There is a motivation in community. Studying with friends might be a good alternative to doing it alone.

Get perspective. You're at seminary. Do you know what a gift that is? Do you know how many third world pastors are pouring themselves out for their people and will never have the opportunity for formal theological education? Be grateful, and work hard.

Repent. Jesus Christ did not die on the cross for your sins so you could avoid work. Live worthy of the calling you have received.

"Walk in a manner worthy of the Lord, fully pleasing to him: bearing fruit in every good work and increasing in the knowledge of God" (Colossians 1:10, ESV).

28

Stumbling at Seminary: Sexual Sin

Your personal sexual integrity will make or break your ministry. A pastor friend of mine put it this way: "Sexual sin among ministers is the atomic bomb." Nothing else can destroy so much, so fast. It will wreak havoc and destruction in the church on a scale that nothing else can.

> "But among you there must not be even a hint of sexual immorality, or of any kind of impurity, or of greed, because these are improper for God's holy people" (Ephesians 5:3, NIV).

Sexual integrity, I contend, is more important than theological integrity. Theological error can be corrected in the process of ongoing ministry, as in the ministry of Apollos (Acts 18:24-26). I laid a few theological eggs myself early in my ministry. I wince to think about them. But those errors are recoverable. A failure of sexual integrity, however, almost always slams the door to ministry.

I remember a young man who came to my church as youth pastor right after I'd left to go to college. He'd been at it for three or four months when I received word of his failure. He had fondled a couple of the girls in the youth group. Boom, just like that, his ministry was over. Makes me wonder what he's doing now. Building maintenance? Insurance? Who knows?

Think of your pastor. Which of the following three sins would provoke the strongest reaction from your church if he were found to have committed it?

- Lying to the finance committee about his expenditures
- Losing his temper and cussing someone out at a ballgame
- Shopping at an adult bookstore

Now answer this: which one would the press jump on?

You see? It's the atomic bomb.

Several years ago, every TV news station in our area showed up at my church because one of our occasional church attenders committed a sex crime. It had nothing to do with our church or its leadership, but they came anyway, and they were on the hunt. The 5:00 news reports called him our "youth pastor."

We must remember that the reputation of Christ is on the line.

Many capable authors have written books on sexual sin, so rather than try to write one of my own, I'll offer just a few suggestions.

Commit to biblical sexual integrity.

Living chastely is, in my opinion, the largest challenge of the Christian life in our culture. Think of all the people who would be willing to become Christians if there were no sexual restrictions! Are you fully, wholeheartedly committed to living chastely in thought and action, limiting all your sexual activity to the secure confines of holy marriage?

If not, maybe ministry isn't for you.

Read this sentence very slowly: Sexual integrity means no pornography.

It's everywhere. Get a filter, get accountability, do whatever you have to do, but stay away. It is deadly to your soul.

Hedges in relationships

Whether you're single or married, it is important for you to have boundaries you enforce in relationships with the opposite sex. Typical boundaries with members of the opposite sex include things like not meeting alone with them behind a closed door, not dining alone with them, not riding alone in a car with them. Take care about your conversation, as well. Be respectful, not flirtatious. Include the other's spouse in conversation and community whenever possible. Be particularly wary of electronic communications. That later than usual text or direct message can lead to bad places in a hurry. A pastor friend of mine was fired for inappropriate texting with another man's wife.

Josh Dix, a leadership coach, writes,

> "If she's not your wife, then she's not yours to touch, love, know the intimate emotions of, call late at night, write emotional emails or flirtatious texts to, or daydream about. She's not yours. She belongs to another man, if not the one she's married to then the one she will marry. She belongs to God. So do you. If you are toying with any of the things I just mentioned–calling, texting, emailing, or even daydreaming about a woman who is not your wife–you are playing with fire. Rest assured, if you continue, it will spread and burn every square inch of your life."[xii]

You also need to be careful with minors, regardless of gender. Don't be alone with kids or teens in ministry situations. One voiced accusation, even if it's false, can set off a firestorm of panic and distrust that can devastate the church and wreck your career.

Have standards for media consumption

Do you have a standard for movies or TV that you will not watch because of its sexual content? No? Then you should get one. There are Netflix series you simply don't need to see. Our culture doesn't blink at highly sexualized programming, but we should. Pick something else. Change the channel.

Learn to Confess

Okay. Everyone who wants to share their most secret, depraved thoughts with someone else, raise your hand. Anyone? That's what I thought. Me neither.

Real accountability for sexual integrity is hard. The last thing I ever want to do is confess my sin. I want to confess my sexual sin last of all. Confession, however, is the path to freedom. Drag it into the light and it loses its power over you. If you're in the grip of temptation, find a trusted friend in Christ, and confess.

Extras:

Go to seminarysurvivalguide.com/book-extras for extra resources.

WHAT SEMINARY MAY NOT TEACH YOU

29
Deciding Where You Stand

There are lots of debatable issues in theology and the practice of ministry. Average church members aren't required to have fully developed theological opinions on these matters. They are usually asked to agree with and support the theological stance of their church, but aren't expected to explain or defend those positions.

Churches, however, expect their leaders to think through and have opinions on a wide range of issues in ministry and theology.

Seminary is a great place to begin to formulate these positions for yourself. You probably arrived at seminary with some issues already firmly settled in your mind. But for ones you've not yet considered, or have yet considered thoroughly, seminary allows you to study the range of positions, pick one to defend, duke it out with professors and fellow students who disagree, and possibly change your mind.

Theological positions can be staked out pretty quickly, but convictions aren't developed overnight. It takes time, prayer, and careful thought. You may not develop strong convictions on every debatable issue. In fact, a leader might be better off with a few carefully chosen convictions than with many. But make no mistake: your convictions will shape and fuel your entire ministry.

Here are some issues in theology and ministry to think deeply about:

- The authority of Scripture, especially how it relates to tradition, reason, and experience.
- Is the canon of Scripture open or closed?
- Charismatic gifts: tongues, healings, miracles
- Baptism of the Holy Spirit
- The role of women in the church and in ministry. Are you complementarian or egalitarian?
- Church governance: where should the functional authority in the church be located? Pastors, bishops, elders, deacons, trustees, or congregation?
- Understanding of election. In many churches, Calvinism and the doctrines of grace are becoming a controversial flashpoint.
- Church discipline: when and how should it be exercised?
- Homosexuality and Same-Sex Marriage: what will your pastoral approach be to homosexual people?
- Gender identity and transgender issues

- Abortion, stem cell research, euthanasia, capital punishment, and other life issues.
- Politics: what stance toward political issues will you take as a Christian leader? What stance should the church take?
- Weddings: for whom will you perform weddings (or not)?
- Divorce and remarriage: what is permissible?
- Counseling: who will you provide pastoral counseling to? How much time will you give to that ministry?
- Baptism: who is a candidate? What mode is proper? How does baptism relate to church membership? Should alien immersion be accepted? What are its limits?
- Communion/The Lord's Supper: What is its meaning? Should communion be open or closed?
- Church membership: requirements and expectations
- Eschatology/Millennial Views. (This is probably not as important to many churches as it used to be.)
- Translations of Scripture: Do you have a preferred translation of the Bible and why?
- Priority and focus of the ministry of the church: What things should the church be and do? What is most important?

When you interview with churches for ministry positions, they will want to know where you stand on these things. Seminary is the time to start figuring it out.

30
Navigating Seminary as a Woman

While most seminarians are men, as are most seminary professors, women make up a significant portion of the seminary community. The Association of Theological Schools reports that women account for around a third of students at all seminaries, and about a fifth of the student body at evangelical seminaries.

Women at seminary report that the environment can be challenging, particularly in seminaries or denominations that hold a complementarian position on gender roles. There, women meet occasional overt opposition their presence at seminary. More often, they face subtle suggestions that women can't or shouldn't lead in ministry.

At the same time, even in complementarian contexts, there is increasing openness to freeing women with leadership gifting to pursue their calling in the church.

The following suggestions are based on input from a survey of women in seminary and personal interviews with women serving in ministry.

Be absolutely sure of your calling.

Women called to ministry have, in the words of one veteran ministry leader, an "uncommon heart." Women, even more than men, need to lean heavily on their sense of calling to ministry. You need a strong internal sense of call, one you can feel deep in your bones. This inner sense also needs to be affirmed and recognized externally, by other believers. In moments of opposition, frustration or self-doubt, the inner conviction and outer affirmation that God wants you in ministry will be your anchor.

Expect to encounter critics. In seminary, some raw students will wield a male leadership standard to establish their theological credentials or to win an argument. People who hold a mature conviction that God wants men leading his church, however, will realize that standard is not a blanket exclusion of the leadership of godly women, as even a cursory reading of the New Testament will demonstrate. Women who are residential students seem to encounter criticism more often than distance or online students.

Many female ministry veterans gave the same advice: "Do not be intimidated." Rest in your calling. Stay the course. You do not have to explain or defend your calling to anyone. Ignore others and focus on your own preparation. If God has called you, then he has a place of ministry for you. There are some churches that will not have you, but that's ok. You wouldn't want to serve there anyway.

Find Community

There will be people at your seminary who value and appreciate the gifts and callings of women, and who are sympathetic to the unique challenges you face. These friends might be fellow students or a professor or other staff member. You will likely find support at your local church. Assemble for yourself an encouragement squad.

Advocate for Yourself

Many times, seminary classes will be taught in a way that focuses on male students aspiring to be preachers or lead pastors. It's a bias of sorts that neglects other people and callings, particularly women.

Press past that neglect and advocate for yourself and others like you. Raise your hand and ask your professor to suggest applications for women in ministry leadership. Ask questions. Speak up. First, it will benefit you and other female students. Beyond that, it will benefit others in the class as well. Virtually all of the men in these classes will have women as part of their future ministry teams. Your perspective and input can help prepare them to lead female leaders. Additionally, you may challenge your professor to think through the application portions of his class more effectively.

Develop Solid and Clear Convictions

Many of the women responding to our survey exhorted women to think clearly and carefully through the Bible's teaching on gender roles. The more prominent and effective your leadership, the more often the issue will come up and you'll be asked to explain your position. Women need to be prepared to offer a thoughtful, biblical theology of gender and leadership.

Priorities and Seasons

Women face a more acute struggle than men when trying to balance family life and ministry, because in most (but not all) families, they are the primary nurturer of kids and the primary administrator of the household. Married women especially, need to order their priorities according to their season of life. One ministry leader suggested that women in the early years of family life who are bearing and raising young children, might need to de-prioritize ministry or seminary during that season. Balance, she said, is the wrong way to think about it. It is a matter of priority. If you are raising young children, it may be a time where ministry needs to drop lower on your list of priorities. As your kids grow and become more independent, ministry can rise to a higher priority.

Lead like a Woman

The most successful women in leadership do not try to lead like men. One woman in ministry I know leads a small army of male volunteers — the burly, truck-driving type — but empowers them not by emasculating them or trying to out-man them, but by appealing to their manliness. She's secure in her identity as a woman, and celebrates their identity as men. They'll do anything she tells them to. It's remarkable.

If you can, find a woman who has successfully led in ministry to mentor you.

Don't Be Discouraged

The church needs godly women leaders who are deeply theologically grounded. I commend you for taking the uncommon step to pursue seminary education. Press on, secure in your calling, and trust God to guide you at each step.

31
Learn to Share the Gospel

When I was in seminary, I didn't share my faith much. Looking back, I believe there were two main reasons.

First, I was unclear about the gospel. That is, I knew what the gospel was, but I was not prepared to express it clearly or concisely. Seminary didn't help. The more I learned about the riches of Old Testament theological backgrounds and their New Testament fulfillments, the more cumbersome and lengthy my gospel explanations became.

Today, thankfully, there is a much stronger emphasis in the church on the clarity and simplicity of the gospel. There are still influential books and ministries, however that teach an approach to evangelism heavily freighted with theological complexity. Seminary students are prone to complicating the gospel because of all they are learning.

Second, I was nervous about talking with strangers about the gospel. Part of my anxiety sprang from not being comfortable with who I was in Christ. In addition to a strong fear of rejection, I also had some negative experiences with my early attempts at evangelism. At a college beach evangelism project, the very first guy I ever tried to share with got violently angry with me. I thought he was going to punch my lights out.

Christian leaders, of all people, need to be proficient at evangelism. Seminary students are becoming authorities on the Christian faith. You should be able to articulate the gospel quickly and clearly. Church members will bring their friends and children to you and expect you to lead them to faith.

There's a larger reason, too. The church today has been ousted from the centers of political and social power. Many writers are now exploring what it will mean to be the church from the margins of society.[xiii] Western societies are now post-Christian and need to be re-evangelized, which will require continual, abundant seed sowing. It will require tens of thousands of Christians having millions of gospel conversations.

Here are a few suggestions from a non-expert evangelist:

Thoroughly master a concise method for presenting the gospel. There are dozens you could use. My church is using the 3 circles illustration, with great success. It's simple, can be learned quickly, and has been adapted for use in multiple languages. There are others: *The Four Spiritual Laws*, the Roman Road, and *Steps to Peace with God* are all classic ways of sharing the gospel. Pick one, memorize it, and practice it dozens of times.

Get good at sharing a *short* version of your testimony. Bill Hybels, in *Just Walk Across the Room*, recommends that your testimony-summary last less than a minute. He argues that if you give people just a taste of it, it allows them room to ask more questions if they are interested. Even better, try the 15-second testimony (Google it!). The point of sharing your testimony is not to force people to listen to your life story, but just to see if they are interested in spiritual conversation. If not, move on.

Count Conversations, Not Conversions. One of my misconceptions about evangelism was that if I didn't actually lead someone "over the line" I was failing. Oh, how wrong I was. Most people need multiple exposures to the gospel in different ways before they believe. Any conversation in which any aspect of the gospel comes up is a win, and we should count it as a win.

Spend time with people far from God. This is a challenge in a residential seminary environment especially, because you're cocooned. Get outside of the seminary bubble. Go to the marketplace and meet some people far from God. Find a way to be a regular in their lives.

This habit is important to learn, because local church ministry tends to keep us surrounded and busy with other believers. Develop the habit of getting out of the Christian ghetto now.

Keep it simple. Especially in seminary, where you're learning all these fancy terms, you'll be tempted to talk way over people's heads. Don't. If you're jazzed about the intricacies of the atonement, it's a good discipline to keep your gospel language simple. I'll go a step further: if you can't explain the gospel in 60 seconds, you don't understand it.

Practice. Find people who do door-to-door or street evangelism, and go shadow them, especially if it makes you uncomfortable or it's "not your style." One of the most helpful things I've done recently is hit the streets with a missionary who is starting house churches. Every day he's trying to start gospel conversations with random people he meets. Spending time doing it with him has demystified the process and removed much of my reluctance and fear.

Use the early offer of prayer. When you meet new people, offer to pray for them in your very first conversation. "I pray all the time. Is there anything I can be praying for you?" People open to prayer are often open to the gospel as well.

Take personal responsibility for your city. Do a quick look at the demographic reports for your city or county. How many people are disengaged from church or far from God? In the county where I live, 1.2 million people are far from God. Find your number, write it down, and ask yourself, "How many of them will hear the gospel today?"

Remember your role. If the fruit is unripe, you don't have to pick it. Some people are ready to receive the gospel, but most are not. If you encounter resistance, it's ok. Most people have to hear the gospel many times before they are ready to receive it. Do what Jesus and the apostles did: if they aren't ready, just move on.

Pray for the lost. Make prayer for the lost part of your daily time with God. Develop a list of five to ten people who are not believers, that you have regular contact with, and pray regularly for them.

Train others to share the gospel. Church leaders cannot be the only ones active in evangelism. The most gifted evangelists in your congregation will most likely be people other than you. If you give them gospel tools and experiences, however, it can ignite their latent gifts, release them into the harvest, and produce a steady stream of new converts to grow the church.

> **Extras:**
>
> Go to <u>seminarysurvivalguide.com/book-extras</u> for extra resources on evangelism, including tools and book recommendations.

32
Learn to Love People

Seminary cannot teach you to love people. If you're going to shepherd people, however, you need to learn to love them.

Albert Mohler, the president of The Southern Baptist Theological Seminary, commented,

> "I don't think in a classroom you can learn what it means to love people the way the Apostle Paul talks about it. I think you have to learn that in the local church. You have to learn that at the bedside of a saint who is going home to be with the Lord, you have to learn that in talking to a couple that thinks divorce is an option and you've got to tell them it isn't. You have to learn this the hard way."[xiv]

In short, seminary classes will not hand you a heart of compassion. It's not in the curriculum. You must get one yourself, elsewhere.

I suspect that most people, if asked to choose between a pastor of uncommon intellect and one of uncommon love, will choose the latter. Jesus was the most brilliant man who ever walked the earth, but it was his evident compassion that drew people to him. If we want to lead well in ministry, we must emulate Him.

Here are a few suggestions:

Pray for a heart of love. Let's be honest. We need supernatural transformation to be capable of this calling. Ask for it.

Get involved in a local church. In a classroom, it's easy to have noble ideas about loving people until it's time to actually do it. Then you run into the scandal of particularity: "Sure I love people. But him? Her?" It's one thing to be prepared to love God's church, until you meet them. Loving that pushy, troublemaking woman is a challenge. Loving that cranky deacon who never has anything good to say is a challenge. Loving the 3rd grader from the abusive home who is too afraid to respond to you is hard.

If you don't know this yet, learn it now: church people are frequently demanding, hardheaded, unreasonable, and unforgiving. They are fallen sinners, just like you.

Who loves people like that anyway? God does.

So start now. Get to know real people in a local church.

Worship as you study. Take time to step back from the up-close scrutiny of God and His Word, and marvel at all He is and all He's done. Abide in His love. Be sure you aren't just parsing verbs during your quiet times.

Love the ones you're with. Are you loving your wife and kids well? If you're single, what about your roommates or friends in the dorm? Begin there.

Find loving people and spend time with them. Find a compassionate pastor or deacon and go on hospital visits with them. Learn to love as you watch them. Have dinner with them and see how they treat their families.

Take up the responsibility. Who in your life, could you demonstrate your love toward? Who's going to love that solitary guy at work? Who's going to love your kid's first grade teacher or your elderly neighbor? Answer: you are. Find ways to do it.

Learn and practice the five love languages. Gary Chapman's book has helped me to expand my vocabulary of love, and gives me a range of options to think about when it's time to express love. Here they are: words of affirmation, acts of service, physical touch, quality time, and gifts.

Practice gratitude. Make thanksgiving a regular part of your time with God. So many times our difficulty loving others springs from our sense of neediness. Gratitude is a way of remembering that in Christ we have all things. Take a moment now: I bet you can fill up a page in a couple of minutes about all you have to be thankful for.

Focus on what you have in common with others. Our failures in communication and compassion for others come when we focus on the things that separate us. You can love people very different from you if you remember a few simple things.

- Like me this person is human, and makes mistakes.
- Like me, this person can fall into the trap of thinking about himself or herself first.
- Like me, this person has needs that only God can fill.
- Like me, this person is deeply loved by Jesus Christ.

33
Ministry Is for Broken People

People have many reasons for going into ministry, some related to their divine calling, but there are human factors as well.

It is widely unacknowledged that personal brokenness motivates many people to pursue vocational ministry. I've never met anyone in ministry who didn't have some level of emotional wounding in their lives. In Henri Nouwen's words, we are "wounded healers."

Emotional wounds make us more sensitive to and responsive to the working of God in our lives. Like Jacob, the wound causes us to stop wrestling and start clinging (Genesis 32). Properly acknowledged and brought to the feet of Christ, our hurt can be a great vehicle for blessing to others (2 Corinthians 1).

These wounds come in many shapes and sizes:

- Strained relationships with parents, especially those who are physically or emotionally absent
- Alcohol or drug abuse, in us or our families
- Traumatic experience
- Early or unexpected loss of a close friend or relative
- Sexual abuse
- Experiences of rejection, isolation or loneliness
- Some other addictive habit or besetting sin
- Physical handicaps

The important question is, where are *you* broken? What are your emotional wounds?

Brokenness has a couple of snares. First of all, the same emotional need that drives us to God can easily drive us to sin. We will be tempted to find quick satisfaction and relief from pain in a forbidden distraction. Many people in ministry flip back and forth between pursuing their healing in Christ, and pursuing some relief in alcohol, pornography, relational dependency, or escapism of other kinds. Unchecked by healthy accountability, this snare can easily lead to moral failure and the end of your ministry.

The second snare is far worse. It is very possible to be driven to Christ by your emotional wounds, and then fail to fully apply to gospel to them. Ministry can become a hiding place from reality. When we hide our wounds from the gospel, they will fester, turn poisonous, and seep out everywhere.

I remember the first time I recognized this reality. I knew two individuals in one church who wore their spiritual passion on their sleeves. Casual visitors to the church thought these two were the godliest people in the congregation. One was a man who was deeply committed to prayer, ready to serve, and always very enthusiastic. As I got to know him, I discovered that his prayerfulness was a cloak for massive spiritual pride that annoyed his wife and drove his children away from Christ.

The second was a woman — passionate, eager, hard-working, and idealistic. Her fervor covered a deep father-wound that manifested itself in the manipulation of others, the undermining of those in authority over her, and a need for control that bordered on insanity. These two people, who on the surface appeared to have it all together spiritually, were in reality the most emotionally messed up people in that church. Their loud displays of commitment to Christ were not sufficient to counteract the bitter poison of an untreated wound.

If we are to have an enduring ministry, we must steward our brokenness well.

The gospel of Jesus is the ultimate solution to our emotional wounds and our proclivity to sin. Stewarding our brokenness means

- Fully acknowledging our wounds
- Pursuing healing and satisfaction in Christ
- Submitting to regular accountability in healthy community

My work with men in recovery has made me more sensitive to how deep emotional wounding can be.

Here are a few things I've learned:

Do not trust your own self-evaluation. My growing conviction is that we are constitutionally incapable of self-knowledge. Like looking at the top of our nose, understanding our own souls is difficult, because it's too close. We have to invite others in to help us understand ourselves.

Community is essential. Church leaders are often isolated and friendless, and feel they have to appear perfect, free from struggle or pain. The wisest and possibly most difficult thing for a pastor is to find a few trusted friends with whom he can be completely transparent. Friends can hear confessions and apply the grace of God to your wounds. The prayers of others might be the most powerful means of liberation we can find.

Do you feel like no one else can understand your brokenness? Do you fear the opinions and rejection of others? Don't be discouraged. The truth is, we are all wounded. God uses just the point of our wounds as a means of blessing to others.

Questions to Ponder:

- How are you emotionally wounded, and how does it affect you?
- How are you pursuing your healing in Christ?
- Who is asking you about it on a regular basis?

Extras:

Go to seminarysurvivalguide.com/book-extras for extra resources.

34
When You Should Quit

For some, the moment will come when the hardships of seminary turn out to be too much. When you're working two jobs, your wife is struggling with a chronic illness, a tragedy happens in your family, or the exhaustion catches up with you, the choices get real. Some will have to take a break. Some will have to shift into low gear and settle for the part-time, 10-year plan. One man who graduated with me when I got my doctorate took *15 years* to complete his Master of Divinity! Some will have to look into online options or even abandon seminary altogether.

Seminary today is a less viable option for aspiring ministers than it was a generation ago. Most pastors throughout the world, of course, never get to go to seminary, but sadly, even in the United States, the barriers, primarily economic, are mounting. Even while I hope for these trends to be reversed, other pathways to theological education and ministry preparation are beginning to spring up. I know many men and women who prepare for ministry and serve effectively without ever making it to or through seminary. If seminary proves to be too much for you, know that you have other legitimate options: personal mentoring leading to ordination in the local church, residency programs, and other alternatives.

If you're thinking of quitting, here are some questions to consider:

Has a major event occurred that changed your life dramatically? A job change, major illness, or death can change the game for families whether they are in seminary or not. Sometimes we think that soldiering on is always the answer, but sometimes life changes so much that struggling on is not the best choice, and could be damaging.

Would you start seminary today? If you weren't already in seminary, would you start your program today, given your life circumstances? If not, that could be a sign that you should downshift.

Is the toll of seminary on your life sustainable? If you are working three jobs and only sleeping 4 hours a night, how long can you keep that up? A month? A semester? Can you carry your current burden to the end of the program?

You cannot run a marathon with the same all-out effort required by a sprint. Seminary can feel like a marathon, but it is more like a long march to a battle. After a marathon, you're done; but after seminary, it's off to ministry. When you're marching to battle, you must pace yourself so that when you're finished, you have the strength to fight. If the road to graduation completely exhausts you, will you even want to pursue ministry when you're done?

How close are you to graduating? If you only have a semester or two left, your answer will be quite different than if you have seven semesters remaining.

Is relief in sight? Can you anticipate a new job or promotion? Recovery from a surgery? If you're in a tough season that will only last weeks or months, you might power through or take a break. But if you are struggling with no relief in sight, the burden can lead to despair.

Can you downshift? Before you quit altogether, consider your options. Can you switch to a shorter degree? Can you scale back to part-time? Will online or distance options make your situation more bearable? Would taking one or two semesters off help?

Is your husband or wife ok with you continuing? Families do seminary *together*. If your spouse thinks you should pause or exit, you had better pay attention.

Have you discussed your situation with anyone? "Plans fail for lack of counsel, but with many advisors, they succeed" (Proverbs 15:22). Don't make major decisions without godly counsel. Consult your pastor, family, and close friends.

What exactly is God calling you to do and be? Revisit your calling to ministry and ask yourself whether seminary is essential to that calling, important to it, or just a nice addition. Remember that seminary is a means, not an end. In times of struggle, it pays to revisit and clarify exactly how seminary relates to God's calling on your life. Leaving seminary doesn't mean you've abandoned your calling.

Seminary is hard, harder than most students expect it to be. If you find you need to slow down, take a break, or abandon it altogether, don't lose heart. Many quality men and women have had to do the same. Seminary is not ultimate — the glory of God and His Kingdom are ultimate. Most godly men and women in history, in fact, have served faithfully and never gone to seminary.

On the other hand, you shouldn't quit just because it's hard. Seminary prepares you for the demands of ministry, and many students need to become accustomed to bearing up under that pressure in order to be ready to serve the church. If leading God's people was easy, everyone would do it.

Whatever you decide: press on, work hard, and honor Jesus.

> Therefore, my dear brothers and sisters, stand firm. Let nothing move you. Always give yourselves fully to the work of the Lord, because you know that your labor in the Lord is not in vain.
>
> 1 Corinthians 15:58 (NIV)

Acknowledgements

Thanks are due to the many friends and advisors who spoke into this book along way. Several generous colleagues read early drafts and offered suggestions: Aaron Smith, David Lee, Charles Campbell, Tim Akin, and Carrie Campbell. Others lent expertise and support along the way: Steve Wright, Tyler Wright, Bev Bonner, Seth Carter, Chris Bonts, Jon Akin, Peyton Jones, Art Rainer, Chuck Lewis, Mark Coppenger, Danny Akin, Dakota Whipple, Bud George, and Trevin Wax.

Special thanks are due to Travis Peterson, Ed Eubanks, and Daryl Eldridge, who were early supporters of and contributors to seminarysurvivalguide.com

Further Resources

Bonus Chapters

Go to seminarysurvivalguide.com/book-extras for bonus chapters, extra reports, and links to resources from select chapters.

About the Author

Mark Warnock, the founder and editor of Seminary Survival Guide (seminarysurvivalguide.com), manages the worship department at Family Church in West Palm Beach, and trains bivocational church planters for the Family Church Network. He teaches courses on worship ministry at Palm Beach Atlantic University. He earned his M.Div. at Southwestern Baptist Theological Seminary, and a Ph.D in Christian Philosophy from The Southern Baptist Theological Seminary. Mark is a classically trained pianist, a World War II enthusiast, and a scuba diver.

Twitter: @markwarnock

Instagram: @mwarnock37

Notes

[i] American Heritage Dictionary

[ii] Caroline Webb, guest on The Art of Manliness Podcast, Episode #214, "How to Have a Good Day, Every Day."

[iii] This approach adapted from Richard Koch, *The 80/20 Principle*.

[iv] http://www.nytimes.com/2013/10/06/business/financial-literacy-beyond-the-classroom.html.

[v] David Cooper, *Repurposing Your Life* (2004), 86-87.

[vi] http://www.goingtoseminary.com/2012/04/02/can-you-go-to-seminary-debt-free/

[vii] http://www.patheos.com/blogs/christiancrier/2013/12/15/average-pastor-salaries-in-united-states-churches/

[viii] https://www.pensions.org/availableresources/bookletsandpublications/documents/clergyeffectivesalaries_2014.pdf

[ix] http://www.nielsen.com/us/en/insights/reports/2016/the-total-audience-report-q1-2016.html, https://www.nytimes.com/2016/07/01/business/media/nielsen-survey-media-viewing.html?_r=0

[x] John Piper, Preaching as Worship: Meditations on Expository Exultation, Bernard H. Rom Lectures in Preaching at Trinity Evangelical Divinity School, November 2-3, 1994.

[xi] Since most evangelical seminarians are male, I'm directing these suggestions to men with respect to their wives for simplicity's sake. Female seminary students with non-student husbands, however, can easily adapt these ideas.

[xii] https://joshdix.wordpress.com/2009/07/06/if-shes-not-your-wife-repent/

[xiii] My thinking has been shaped most significantly by *The Benedict Option* by Rod Dreher, and *You Are What You Love* and *How (Not) to Be Secular* by James K.A. Smith.

[xiv] Jeff Robinson, "Trustees: Mohler: Pastors Needs Tender Side," Baptist Press, October 17, 2007, http://www.bpnews.net/26626/trustees-mohler-pastors-need-tender-side.

CPSIA information can be obtained
at www.ICGtesting.com
Printed in the USA
LVHW052359040520
654936LV00008B/2610

9 781977 817891